KEYS TO THE PAST

KEYS TO THE PAST

Archaeological Treasures of Mackinac

Lynn L. M. Evans

Mackinac Island, Michigan

Keys to the Past
Archaeological Treasures of Mackinac

By Lynn L.M. Evans
Curator of Archaeology
Mackinac State Historic Parks

Design by Group 230, Lansing
Object photography by John Wooden

Mackinac State Historic Parks
PO Box 370
Mackinac Island, Michigan 49757

 Library of Congress Cataloging-in-Publication Data

Evans, Lynn L. M., 1965-
  Keys to the past : archaeological treasures of Mackinac / Lynn L.M.
Evans.-- 1st ed.
     p. cm.
Includes bibliographical references (p.).
  ISBN 0-911872-85-X (hardcover) -- ISBN 0-911872-84-1 (pbk.)
 1. Mackinaw City Region (Mich.)--Antiquities. 2. Mackinac Island
(Mich. : Island)--Antiquities. 3. Material culture--Michigan--Mackinaw
City Region. 4. Material culture--Michigan--Mackinac Island (Island)
5. Historic sites--Michigan--Mackinaw City Region. 6. Historic
sites--Michigan--Mackinac Island (Island) 7. Excavations
(Archaeology)--Michigan--Mackinaw City Region. 8. Excavations
(Archaeology)--Michigan--Mackinac Island (Island) 9. Mackinaw City
Region (Mich.)--History, Local. 10. Mackinac Island (Mich. :
Island)--History, Local. I. Mackinac State Historic Parks. II. Title.
  F574.M17E93 2003
  977.4'923--dc22
                              2003017500

First Edition
First Printing   2,000 copies, soft cover
                    1,000 copies, hard cover

Printed in the United States of America

TABLE OF CONTENTS

This book was made possible by a generous grant from
Mackinac Associates in honor of their twentieth anniversary.

INTRODUCTION

STORIES UNCOVERED

"Take out the trash!" "Where did I lose that button?" "Don't let your pennies drop through those floor boards son!"
"Put that fish out on the compost pile." "Did you break that window?"

Every day we leave a trail of materials behind us, deliberately or by accident. Some of the items that we discard are hauled away, others disappear, and a few are just forgotten. Our lives are filled with artifacts and we leave many behind as we go about the business of living. Broken glass or ceramics, dropped nails, lost buttons or jewelry are annoyances for us but, if uncovered, can become valuable evidence of where we have been and what we have done. Have you ever returned to a place where you used to live and had memories rekindled by seeing again the familiar look of the old kitchen or the well-worn stones of the garden path? The things that we leave behind are rich resources for the archaeologist and historian. Rediscovering them allows us to reconstruct places and memories, and to piece together stories of the past.

Just as we leave behind evidence of our lives, so communities unavoidably mark the land and leave many types of records of their existence and their activity. Easiest to understand are the visual images, such as paintings, drawings, sketches and photographs, films and other moving pictures. Visual images show how things appeared at one time, and can be examined in great detail to help understand the past. Architecture and artifacts often survive over time, and when studied can reveal much about a place and a way of life. Buildings readily show changes made over time, and artifacts can often be dated and understood for how they were made and used, what they cost and where they came from. Documentary evidence is another rich source of information about the past, and includes maps, books, letters and records of great variety. With the growth of the Internet, records from around the world are increasingly available to everyone.

To understand a place and time of long ago, we need evidence from all of these sources and more. No matter how large the pool of available documentary, visual and artifact evidence, there is rarely enough to provide a full view of what life was like long ago. Archaeologists help expand the available evidence by carefully searching in the ground for materials left behind, or for evidence in the soil of "disturbances," things that have changed over time. The Hollywood image of the swashbuckling archeologist making a great discovery is largely fictional, but the real work of archaeology can be as fascinating as the myth and of lasting value.

At Mackinac State Historic Parks, two of the principal historic sites were obliterated from the landscape by the 1900s. The fur trading village and fort at Michilimackinac on the south side of the Straits was burned by the British when they built Fort Mackinac and relocated to Mackinac Island in 1780-81. The site, known today as Colonial Michilimackinac, was covered by shifting beach sand and construction of the village nearby, eliminating all surface evidence of the colonial settlement from view. Artifacts were found from time to time, either as "surface finds" or by "treasure hunters" digging on the site. The villagers recognized the importance of the site, preserving it as a park and donating it to the state of Michigan in 1904 to become Michigan's second state park, under the jurisdiction of the Mackinac Island State Park Commission.

The 1780-1820 industrial complex at Mill Creek declined in productivity, profitability and usefulness with the coming of larger mills elsewhere in Michigan and around the lakes. The buildings deteriorated, collapsed or were removed, leaving no visible evidence of the once busy complex of mill, forge, barn, home and other structures. The mill site was rediscovered in the 1970's by local historians Ellis and Mary Olson, Margaret Lentini and other local residents. In cooperation with the historians of Mackinac State Historic Parks, most of the original land of the mill site was transferred to the Park Commission and developed as Historic Mill Creek.

At both Colonial Michilimackinac and Historic Mill Creek little surface evidence survived to tell the stories of the sites. Archaeology is a key tool used to identify what areas were developed and used by colonial and early American settlers, determine the locations of buildings and reveal how buildings were used and life was lived at the sites. At Fort Mackinac on Mackinac Island, fourteen original historic buildings survive, along with many landscape features that reveal the purpose and operation of fort components. Still, even with this evidence available, archaeology has revealed much about life at Fort Mackinac that was unknown from other evidence.

Archaeology — How does it work?

Archaeology is inherently destructive; once a site is excavated it is gone forever. Archaeologists strive to recover and record every bit of information possible as they excavate. The first step is to know where they are in space. A grid system is established over the site to create horizontal control. At Michilimackinac the same 10' x 10' grid system has been used since 1959 to tie all of the excavations together. Vertical control, how deep things are, is measured from benchmarks of known elevation above sea level.

As archaeologists carefully remove soil using trowels and other tools they are looking not only for artifacts, but also for changes in soil. Differences in soil color and texture may indicate the remains of a building or the presence of a feature such as a trash pit or privy. As archaeologists excavate, they take detailed notes on their findings and draw careful maps showing the relationships of soil types and artifacts to each other. Various types of photographs are taken. In this way the site can be reconstructed on paper or in a computer after the excavation is complete.

These basic data recovery techniques have been refined over time to increase the information gained. The early excavations at Michilimackinac, following the standard practices of the day, used prison laborers to shovel off three-inch layers of soil and run the dirt through quarter-inch mesh screen. Today all excavators are professionally trained archaeologists removing tenth-of-a-foot (1.25") layers by hand and using water to force the soil through window screen. This makes possible recovery of tiny artifacts such as seed beads, lead shot and food remains, including fish bones, fish scales and seeds. These small clues help archaeologists reconstruct a much more complete picture of life at the site.

The recovery of food remains has been particularly helpful in studying the different ethnic groups that lived at Michilimackinac. Cultural background plays a huge role in what people choose to eat. The British wanted to continue to eat familiar, domesticated, "British" food, such as beef, pork and garden vegetables, even if it had to be imported at great expense over long distances. The French, many of whom married into local Native American families, were more adventurous and willing to rely more on locally available foods such as waterfowl, game and berries. Of course everyone ate lots of fish!

Analyses of this sort take lots of time in the laboratory. It takes more time to process and analyze a site than it does to excavate it. Artifacts must be cleaned, labeled with a number identifying the context from which they came, and identified.

The stratigraphy, showing the layers of soil, is re-created on paper. In general, lower layers are earlier than higher layers, but when soil has been moved, historically, to dig a cellar or in modern times, to look for treasure, the levels get mixed up. Once it has been determined in what order the layers were deposited, artifacts are used to date them. A layer can be no older than its youngest artifact. For example, a layer with a 1763 coin has to have been deposited in 1763 or later. Easily dateable artifacts such as coins, military buttons and well-documented ceramic types are particularly useful for this.

Artifacts also help identify how a particular site was used, perhaps as house, shop or church, and whether it was used by rich or poor, civilian or military, and so on. An example of this is the American Millwright's House at Historic Mill Creek. The remains of a double fireplace and artifacts found associated with each side of the hearth show that the west room of the house was a living space, while the east room was used as a blacksmith shop. The house can be dated to the American period by the ceramics found there. Documents reveal that wealthy entrepreneur Michael Dousman owned the property at that time. The artifacts found at the site are solidly middle-class, however, indicating that a hired millwright occupied the house.

WHY ARCHAEOLOGY?

A final but critical step is to make the archaeological information available for use by students, scholars and museum visitors. Mackinac State Historic Parks regularly publishes the results of archaeological excavations, and research papers that utilize archaeological collections. Archaeological Completion Reports are available for purchase. The results of archaeological research help museum staff determine the authentic appearance of historic and reconstructed buildings, and accurately furnish them so that visitors can obtain an accurate picture of the historic sites.

As archaeological methods have improved, the pace of excavation has slowed. More of Colonial Michilimackinac was excavated in 1959 than in the entire decade of the 1990s. As archaeologists have had the opportunity to return to sites partially excavated in the 1960s (the South Southwest Row House at Michilimackinac) and 1970s (the millwrights' houses at Mill Creek) they have seen how much more information can now be recovered. Equal advances in technique can be expected in the next forty years. For that reason the Mackinac Island State Park Commission established archaeological preserves, which will be protected from disturbance now and available for future research and use of yet-undiscovered techniques.

Archaeology teaches us much about the everyday life of the people who lived at the Straits of Mackinac for hundreds of years. In the following pages you will see some of the most spectacular and evocative artifacts excavated by the staff of Mackinac State Historic Parks during the past forty-five years. We hope these images will inspire you to want to learn more about the people of the past, and the wonderful stories that archaeology has helped to reveal about the Straits of Mackinac.

This publication is made possible by the generous support of Mackinac Associates, the membership and support organization for Mackinac State Historic Parks, in honor of the twentieth anniversary of this outstanding group. Through memberships, contribution and fund raising, Associates members support exhibitions, restoration, and events throughout Mackinac State Historic Parks, and make possible Education Outreach programs that take Mackinac stories to classrooms around the state. We are grateful to Mackinac Associates for twenty years of outstanding support.

The Mackinac Island State Park Commission was established in 1895. The seven commissioners are appointed by the Governor and confirmed by the Senate and are charged with stewardship of Mackinac Island State Park, Fort Mackinac, Colonial Michilimackinac and Historic Mill Creek. The commissioners, led for more than a decade by Chairman Dennis O. Cawthorne, are dedicated and enthusiastic in their support of the professional historical, archaeological and museum programs operated since 1958. They have our sincere appreciation for this commitment to preserving the heritage of Mackinac for future generations.

Carl R. Nold

Lynn L. M. Evans

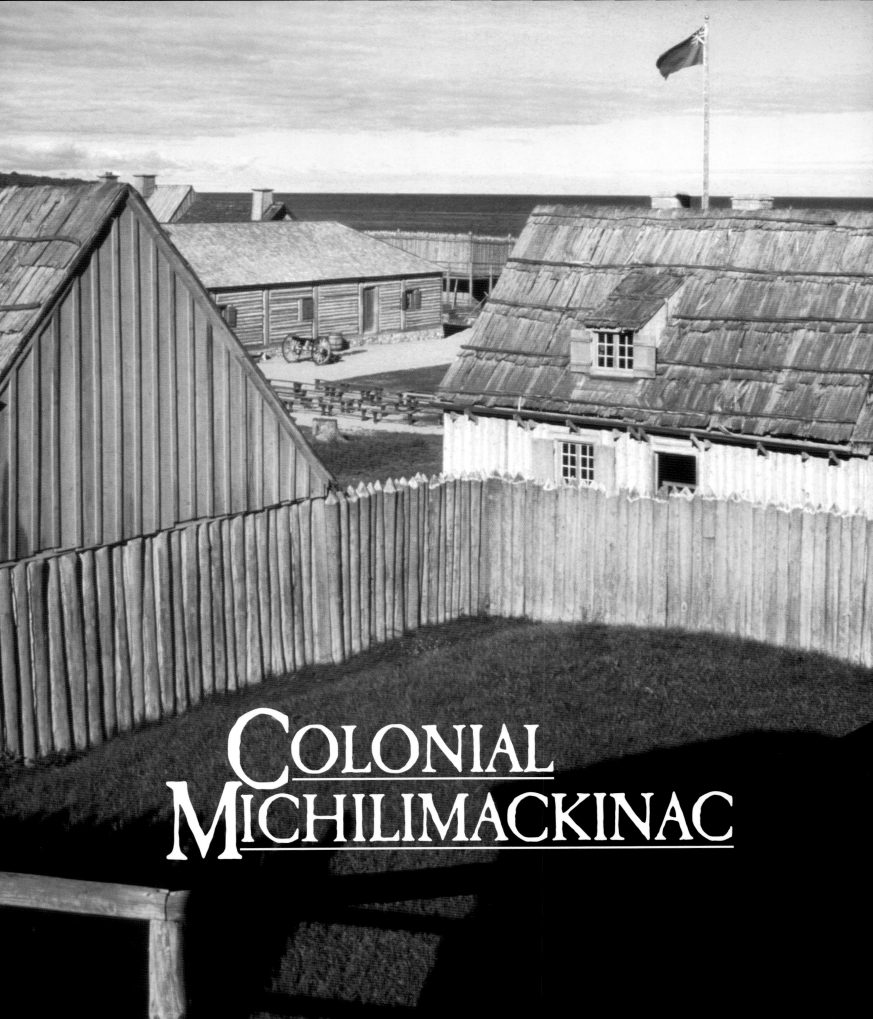

COLONIAL
MICHILIMACKINAC

Powder Magazine

"The powder magazine is buried and covered with turf."
–Michel Chartier de Lotbinière, military engineer, describing Michilimackinac in 1749

The powder magazine was burned during the final demolition of Fort Michilimackinac. Charred wood wall posts and floorboards, seen here as excavated in 1975, were preserved when the sod roof collapsed on them, extinguishing the fire.

The preserved powder magazine from current underground viewing platform. The charred floorboards and wall posts are original.

Solomon-Levy-Parant House

"Before the Royal Notary residing at the post of Michilimackinac, the undersigned were present: Sieur Pierre Parant and Dlle. Marieanne Chaboiller, his wife, who have acknowledged and confessed, by those present, to have sold, ceded, left and transferred . . . to Sieurs Solomon and Levis, merchants in this post…a house belonging to them with its dependances seated and situated in this fort."
–June 29, 1765, Notarial Records

The ruins of the Solomon-Levy-Parant house, shown here being excavated in 1983, were remarkably well preserved. The stones in the foreground are remnants of the hearth. The dark stains beyond the hearth are floorboards. The rocky depression in the rear is the top of the root cellar.

The reconstructed Solomon-Levy-Parant House incorporates the original hearth stones. Ezekiel Solomon and Gershon Levy were among the first Jewish settlers in Michigan.

French Faience Plate

Faience is earthenware covered with a glaze containing lead and tin oxide. The tin oxide creates an opaque white surface that can be painted. Tin-glazed earthenware was produced across Western Europe and known as faience, delft or majolica, depending on its country of origin. National origin is usually determined by the style of decoration.

English Delft Bowl

Chinese-inspired designs, such as the floral pattern on this bowl, were common on tin-glazed earthenware pieces, in imitation of more expensive Chinese porcelain. This bowl was probably manufactured in Lambeth. Tin-glazed earthenware is the most common type of ceramic excavated at Michilimackinac.

Chinese Export Porcelain Saucer

The Chinese invented porcelain before 900 A.D. The best porcelain is so thin as to be translucent. Porcelain was brought to Michilimackinac from China by way of France or England. In the eighteenth century it occupied a status between tin-glazed earthenware and some of the specialty wares. Most of the Chinese porcelain at Michilimackinac is from tea services.

Creamware Cup

Creamware, a thin bodied, lead-glazed, cream-colored earthenware was one of the major achievements in eighteenth-century English ceramic technology. It was developed by 1760 and was a major export item by 1770, making it an excellent time marker for the British period at Michilimackinac.

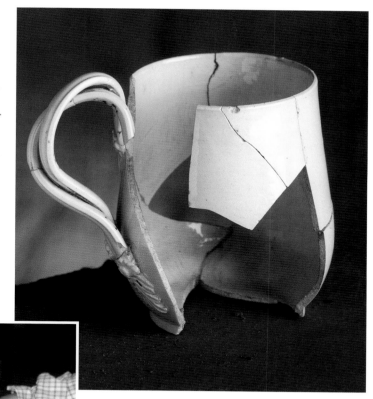

Cooking demonstrations at Michilimackinac take place in reconstructed row houses that are furnished based on archaeological findings. Notice the creamware on the table.

Creamware Platter

"16 Plates Queens Ware"
–John Askin inventory December 31, 1776

Josiah Wedgwood gave Queen Charlotte (wife of George III) a set of his cream-colored earthenware and then marketed similar sets as "Queen's Ware." The double rib and groove, seen on this platter, was the original "Queen's" pattern.

Whieldon-type Teacup

Thomas Whieldon was a pioneering eighteenth-century English potter. He developed this high style tortoise shell glaze, which was then copied by other manufacturers. Tortoise shell glaze usually is found on tea services.

English Red Stoneware Teapot

This teapot is the most unusual ceramic item recovered from Michilimackinac. A distinctive, unglazed, fine grained, red stoneware was developed in England in the late seventeenth century and produced in limited quantities for over one hundred years. The elaborate chinoiserie (a style imitating Chinese motifs) design was stamped onto the pot. It probably was manufactured in Leeds.

Green-Glazed Earthenware Bowl

Coarse earthenware, fired at a low temperature and having little decoration, was the most utilitarian ceramic type at Michilimackinac. It was the cheapest ceramic and used in everyone's kitchen for food preparation. The green glaze on this bowl is typical of French Canadian pottery. Because there was no local pottery industry at Michilimackinac, many dishes were made of pewter, wood and bone.

Case and Wine Bottles

Most bottles came to Michilimackinac containing wine, ale, rum, gin, brandy or other alcoholic beverages. Once there, however, they were reused to hold many kinds of liquids until they broke. The olive green bottles are British in origin, while the blue-green bottle came from the Continent.

Case bottles get their name from their rectangular shape, designed to fit in wooden cases for transport.

Turlington Bottle

By The Kings Royal Patent Granted To Robt. Turlington For His Invented Balsom of Life. London Jany. 26, 1754
–Molded inscription on bottle

Robert Turlington patented a formula to cure "stone, gravel, cholick, and inward weakness" in 1744. The ingredients were: "storax, coriander seeds, aloes, fennell, mastick, cardamums, frankinsence, aniseeds, benjamin, angilica, gum elemy, cinnamon, guiacum, cloves, myrrh, nuttmeggs, araback, winter bark, perue, nettle seeds, tolue, juniper, safron, mace, oyle, Saint john wort, marsh mallows and rectifying spirits." Despite his patent, Turlington was frequently imitated and this may be a counterfeit bottle.

Molded Glass Tankard

Tankards were designed for drinking ale. This tankard was found in a root cellar in the southwest section of the fort. It probably belonged to a wealthy trader. Pewter, tin or ceramic tankards were much more common. This lead glass tankard was about seven inches tall before it was broken.

Engraved Cordial Glass

A cordial glass is a specialized piece of tableware only the wealthy could afford. The flowering plant engraved on this glass makes it even rarer.

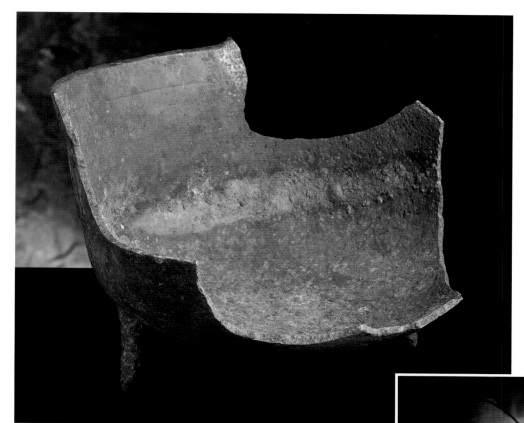

Cast Iron Pot

Pots were a necessity for every household or soldiers' mess. They were used for all manner of soups and stews, basic foods of the day, and for heating water for any purpose.

Soup or stew was the usual main dish at meals at Michilimackinac. A cook could prepare one with whatever meat or vegetables she had on hand, and let it cook while attending to other tasks.

Whitefish Skeleton

"These high prices of grain and beef led me to be very industrious in fishing . . . Whitefish, which exceed the trout as delicious and nutritive food, are here in astonishing numbers . . . Those who live on them for months together preserve their relish to the end."
– Alexander Henry wintering at Michilimackinac, 1761

Although diet varied greatly among the different groups of people at Michilimackinac, everyone ate fish. It was plentiful, readily available and delicious! Fish remains are the most common artifact excavated at Michilimackinac. This fish skeleton was found at the bottom of a refuse pit in the southwest corner of the fort.

Bone Harpoon

*Most fishing was done with nets, because that is the most efficient way to get a large catch. Lines and spears were sometimes used as well. This bone harpoon would have been on the end of a spear. Native Americans made most bone tools. Many French-Canadian traders married local native women. Their children, the **métis** people, learned skills (such as bone technology), languages and cultural traditions from both heritages. The **métis** became the backbone of the fur trade.*

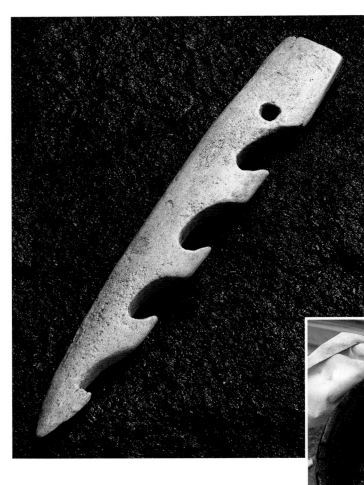

Fish were preserved by smoking and salting.

Chicken Egg

The British tried to maintain their traditional diet as best they could. This chicken egg was found in a privy used by Lieutenant George Clowes and other officers living in the southeast row house to guard the powder magazine in the 1770s.

Red Earthenware Chamber Pot

Chamber pots were a necessity at Michilimackinac where there were few privies or latrines. Using a chamber pot was infinitely preferable to trekking outside on a cold winter night! This chamber pot ranks in between a wooden bucket and very elaborately decorated ceramic chamber pots in style and cost.

Bone Comb

Eighteenth-century standards of personal hygiene were quite different from those of today. Nevertheless bone and horn combs are common on trade inventories. The fine teeth on this comb would be useful in combing out head lice and their eggs.

Bone Syringe

Surgeon's mates Daniel Morison and David Mitchell were the best-trained medical professionals at Michilimackinac. Most healing would have been done by women relying on herbal knowledge passed down through generations. This bone syringe is a sign of the increasingly scientific treatment of medical problems.

8th Regiment Buttons

The 8th or King's Regiment was the final regiment to serve at Michilimackinac, arriving in 1774 and moving the garrison to Fort Mackinac on Mackinac Island between 1779 and 1781. These are some of the 8th button types found at the fort. Enlisted men's buttons were pewter and either plain or had a rope or leafy border. Officers' buttons had brass crowns. The most elaborate one shows the badge granted to the regiment by the King, as the King's Regiment of Foot. In addition to the required 8, it shows the white horse of the Royal House of Hanover and the Crown and Garter with the Latin motto, "HONI SOIT QUI MAL Y PENSE," which means "evil to him who thinks evil."

Today Michilimackinac is interpreted to 1778, its peak before the move to Mackinac Island began. These guides wear the uniform of the Kings 8th Regiment, who garrisoned the post from 1774 to 1784. Notice the Ks8 on their buttons.

10th and 60th Regiment Buttons

The Clothing Warrant of 1768 specified that the buttons on British army coats bear the regimental number. Since we know when various regiments were stationed at Michilimackinac, their regimental buttons serve as excellent time markers. For example, the 60th served from 1766 to 1772 (also from 1761-1763) and the 10th from 1772 to 1774. Styles varied between regiments and also within regiments, with officers' buttons being more elaborate than those of enlisted men.

18th Regiment Button

Sometimes we find buttons from regiments that were never stationed at Michilimackinac. This pewter button is from the 18th or Royal Irish Regiment of Foot. This regiment was stationed in North America from 1767 to 1775, at which time the enlisted men were drafted into other regiments. Fifty-eight men from the 18th were drafted into the 8th at Detroit on July 8, 1776, and some must have been sent from there on to Michilimackinac.

Iron Flintlock Lockplate and Cock

Eighteenth-century firearms, both military and civilian, operated with a flintlock firing mechanism. A small amount of powder was placed in the pan. A sharpened flint was held in the jaws of the cock. When the trigger was pulled, the cock flew forward and the flint hit the frizzen, a hardened piece of steel, creating sparks, which ignited the gunpowder. Some of the fire from the resulting explosion went through a small touchhole and into the barrel to the main powder charge and ammunition. Guns were critical for survival on the Great Lakes frontier for hunting food and furs as well as defense.

Brass Flintlock Sideplate

Eighteenth-century French and British guns fired the same way, but were fitted with different styles of furnishings, making it easy to identify the source of many gunparts. The serpent sideplate was used on British trade guns for over one hundred years beginning around 1775. Sideplates function as washers securing the lockplate screws to the gun.

Brass Flintlock Escutcheons

Some of the gun furniture was elaborately decorated, such as these escutcheons. The crowned escutcheon is from a French trade gun. The escutcheon with the human bust is probably English.

This soldier carries a reproduction "Brown Bess" flintlock musket. The buttplate is visible at the near end of the gun. The wrist escutcheon is visible just above the girl's left hand. The lock mechanism is between her hands.

Brass Flintlock Finials

Sometimes the same design was repeated on several parts of a gun. These "flaming torch" finials are from **fusils fin***, good quality French guns. The finial on the left is from a triggerguard; the finial on the right is from a buttplate.*

Iron Door Handle and Latch

Blacksmiths at Michilimackinac could have made utilitarian hardware, such as this door handle and latch. However, records indicate that most hardware was imported, since it was so expensive to import raw material. The blacksmith spent most of his time repairing metal objects, especially guns.

Window Pane

Although glass had to be imported from Europe, first by ship, then by canoe, the high number of windowpane fragments excavated shows that glass windows were common at Michilimackinac.

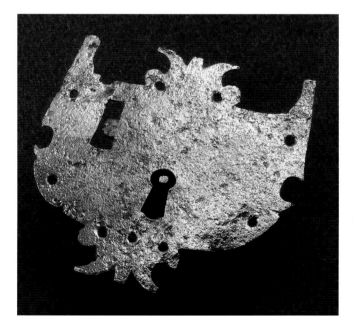

Iron Lock

This lock is from a piece of furniture, rather than a structural door. Chests, armoires, desks and other pieces of furniture could be locked for privacy and security in households with extended family, business partners and servants all living in a few rooms.

Iron Keyhole Escutcheon

The escutcheon is the decorative plate surrounding the keyhole when the lock mechanism is attached from the back. This unusual design may have been matched on other pieces of furniture.

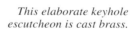

This elaborate keyhole escutcheon is cast brass.

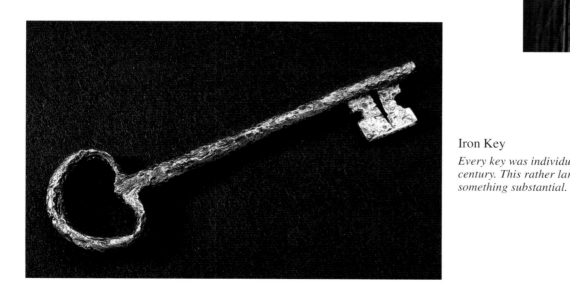

Iron Key

Every key was individually made in the eighteenth century. This rather large key must have unlocked something substantial.

Brass Barrel Band

Gunpowder barrels had brass bands, rather than more common iron bands, because brass was less likely to spark. The arrow on the band identifies it as the King's gunpowder. The arrow was used to mark all sorts of government property, from trees for ships' masts to bedding in the barracks, in the days before most British subjects could read.

Wax Seal

This is part of a wax seal that once closed a letter. It was found in the military latrine. We don't know who "JG" was.

Intaglio Letter Seal

This letter seal may have been discarded because the glass intaglio is cracked. This seal pivots in its holder, unlike the fixed seal shown below.

Intaglio Letter Seal

This seal was used with sealing wax to close correspondence to ensure confidentiality before gummed envelopes. Seals also were used on official documents. Because literacy was rare, artifacts that indicate the ability to write, such as this letter seal, signify high status residents of the houses where they are found. The handle is brass and the intaglio is glass.

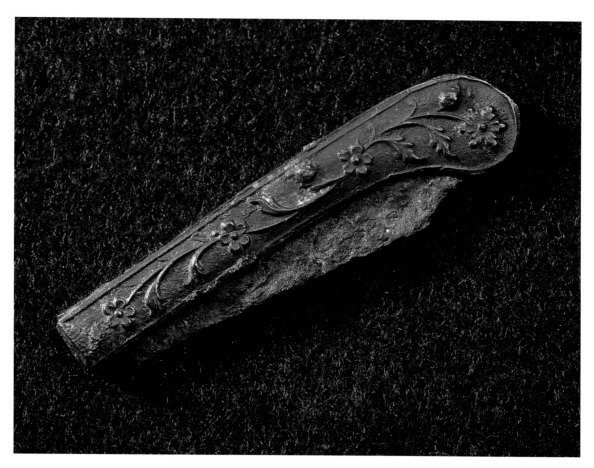

Penknife

Penknives, originally used to sharpen quill pens, suggest a literate owner. In addition to the fancy floral design, tiny traces of red and gold paint are visible on the handle of this one. It must have been a very showy accessory for someone at Michilimackinac.

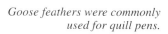
Goose feathers were commonly used for quill pens.

Iron Telescope

The eighteenth century was the Age of Enlightenment, and the spirit of scientific inquiry was common among the educated class. A telescope also had practical uses for navigation and watching for approaching canoe brigades and other vessels.

Bone Sundial Base

Although elegant watches existed in the eighteenth century, a pocket sundial was more practical for the traveler in the days before standardized time zones.

European Coins

Coins were rare on the colonial frontier and are even more rare in the archaeological record. In over forty years of excavation about 30 coins have been found, some too worn to be definitely identified. Due to the scarcity of coins, multiple currencies were used at Michilimackinac. The coin on the top left is an English 1720 George I copper halfpenny. The figure shown is Britannia. The coin on the bottom right is a French 1751 Louis XV two **sou** *coin. A* **sou** *was roughly equivalent to a shilling. The other two coins are Spanish. On the top right is a 1731 Phillip V* **medio real** *(half* **real***), minted in Mexico City. Eight* **reales** *made up one pillar dollar. The final coin is a two bit piece cut from a pillar dollar. The "2"s are overstamps and the reverse side is overstamped with the British broad arrow.*

Brass Spigot

Spigots were used to tap barrels, kegs and casks of wine, brandy, rum and other beverages. These spirits were doled out to soldiers as rations, Native people as presents and voyageurs as provisions, as well as sold for personal use.

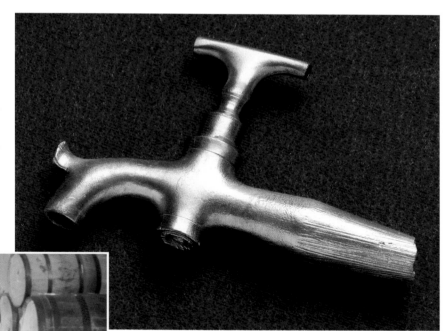

Spirits for rations and official gifts were stored in the King's Storehouse.

Textile Fragment

Fabric of all sorts — linen, cotton, calico, serge, muslin, flannel, stroud, sheeting — was the most common item traded for furs. Unfortunately, very few textiles survived. The salts in copper-wrapped thread preserved the textile fragments we excavate. These metallic trims were used on fancy civilian clothing, as well as military hats and coats.

The Trader's Store at Michilimackinac is stocked with a variety of textiles and other goods available for trade for furs and corn.

Lead Seals

Lead seals were fastened onto bolts of cloth to indicate quality, taxes paid, origin or ownership. The rooster with three fleurs-de-lis was the symbol for cloth inspectors in Mazamet, France. The crocodile chained to the palm tree with letters COL NE was the symbol for Nice, France; the letters are the abbreviation for the Latin name for Nice. The other side of this seal is stamped "3 FILS" for triple-ply stockings. "CDI" stamped between two leafy branches was the mark of the Compagnie des Indes, a maritime trade association.

Brass Buckles

Buckles, buttons, hooks, pins and ties were the options for clothing fasteners in the days before Velcro, zippers and snaps. Like buttons, buckles were often decorative as well as functional. The large buckles probably are from shoes. The medium ones could be from belts for pants or swords, and the smallest might be from knee breeches or garters.

Silver and Brass Buttons

"There was a Pair of Gold Sleeve Buttons left in the Drawer of the Counter, Mr McTavish sold them to a French Man at this place, please to send them up when an opportunity offers"
–James Bannerman (Michilimackinac) to William Edgar (Detroit) June 10, 1776

Button fragments of many types are a common find. Ready-made clothes were scarce in the eighteenth century and most garments were made to order, including choice of trim. Buttons were both decorative and functional.

This couple is dressed for a celebration. Notice the buckled shoes, numerous buttons and fancy trim.

Brass Thimble

"Mrs. Askin begs you to have a gold thimble made for her the same size as that you so kindly sent her before, but much stronger on the edge, the other being broken already in several places."
–John Askin (Michilimackinac) to Richard Dobie (Montreal) June 15, 1778

Thimbles, needles, pins, thread and other sewing accessories were traded along with cloth.

Iron Awl with Bone Handle

"1 Gro[ss] awl Blades"
–David McCrae accounts, Goods for one canoe for M. Landoise

Awls were most commonly used for piercing holes through leather. Imported as blades, the owner could then fashion a bone or wood handle to suit him or herself. This bone handle is especially elaborate. Notice the face on the end of the handle.

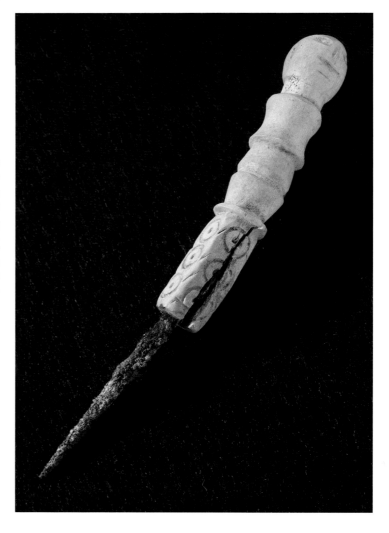

Glass Necklace Beads

"1 Bunch blue Beeds . . .
20 Bunches Mock Garnetts . . .
2 Bunches Beads . . .
1 Bunch long blk beads . . .
17 Bunches Barley Corn beads . . .
1 Bunch Small white Beads . . .
1 Bunch long white Beads . . .
1 Bunch Small round Beads"
–David McCrae accounts, Goods
for one canoe for M. Landoise

Colorful glass beads of all kinds
were popular trade items. Most
were manufactured in Venice.

Man-in-the-Moon Bead

This distinctive bead probably dates to the French
era at Michilimackinac. What, if anything, the man
in the moon symbolized to the French or Native
Americans of the time is unknown today.

Brass Hawk Bell

"The sound of bells and other jingling materials, attached to the women's dresses, enabled them to keep time."
–Alexander Henry, February 1776 trip across Northern Plains

Hawk bells were a common, inexpensive trade item. The name hawk bell comes from their original use in falconry.

Silver Earring

Silver ornaments became increasingly common trade goods throughout the British era at Michilimackinac. The ball and cone design is an early and common form.

Brass Jesuit Rings

*Jesuit missionaries were the earliest Europeans to live in the Upper Great Lakes. They encouraged Native Americans to learn Bible verses and sections of catechism with rewards of beads, rings and other tokens. Early Jesuit rings were cast and had religious symbols. Over the course of the eighteenth century these brass rings lost their religious symbolism and became cheaply made trade items. The ring faces shown are examples of these later designs. The heart with arrows probably comes from Sacred Heart designs. The "LV" may come from an early "L-heart" design representing devotion to Louis, king of France or Loyola, founder of the Jesuit order. The "IXXI" design appears to have evolved from a double M design, for **Mater Misericordia**, Mother of Mercy.*

A small Native American camp is set up outside the Michilimackinac palisade wall. Notice the brass Jesuit rings on the interpreter's hand.

Brass Saint Ignatius Medallion

Brass religious medallions had a personal, rather than trade, meaning. Medals depicting many different saints have been found at Michilimackinac. This medal shows Saint Ignatius of Loyola, founder of the Society of Jesus, better known as the Jesuits. Jesuit missionaries were a vital part of the straits community. The letters surrounding Ignatius are S IGAC FVI DA SOC for Saint Ignatius founder of the Society. Saint Ignatius is shown holding a tablet with the letters AD MAIO. These are the first letters of "Ad Majorem Dei Gloriam," which means "to the greater glory of God," a Jesuit motto. The Virgin Mary is pictured on the reverse side.

Brass Crucifix

Crucifixes could be a component of a rosary or worn separately as jewelry. In the later British period silver crosses were a trade item. In this example the corpus (body of Christ) and cross were cast separately and riveted together. The inscription INRI on the cross is from the Latin for Jesus of Nazareth, King of the Jews.

Rosary

This is the largest section of a rosary found at Michilimackinac. The main circlet consists of 57 small, plain, round ivory beads and four medium, grooved, concave beads, with an additional five beads on the section leading to the missing crucifix. All of the beads are joined by metal links. A standard "Dominican" rosary has only 50 of the small beads and five medium beads. However, there are special rosaries or chaplets, such as the Franciscan Crown Rosary, which have additional beads.

A French-Canadian wedding is re-enacted twice each summer day at the church of Ste. Anne de Michilimackinac. Notice the rosary carried by the priest.

Clay Medallion

This religious medallion, made of fine pink clay, may have been painted at one time. The design is almost certainly of Jesus and Mary. The lip around the front suggests that it was in a setting. This clay medallion is unique in the collection.

Brass Finger Rings

"2 Gro[ss] Stone rings"
–David McCrae accounts, Goods for one canoe for M. Landoise

These rings, with glass stones, could have been used in the fur trade or worn by inhabitants of the fort.

Brass Earring

This fancy earring may have adorned a young French-Canadian girl at Michilimackinac. The style is similar to some cufflinks found at the site. The stones are glass.

Brass Cufflink

Although life on the frontier could be harsh and difficult, officers and prosperous traders at Michilimackinac tried to follow the latest fashions from London and Europe. The stones are glass.

Repaired Cufflink

Michilimackinac was cut off from the world by snow and ice for almost six months every year. When things broke, residents had to make do with what they had. The missing half of this cufflink was replaced with a hawkbell. Reuse and recycling are not new ideas.

Limestone Micmac Pipe

"the pierre à calumet, or pipestone . . . employed for the bowls of tobacco pipes, both by the Indians and Canadians."
–Alexander Henry on 1761 journey to Michilimackinac

Pipestone refers to catlinite, steatite, mudstone and limestone. This pipe is carved from limestone. The three part form of bowl, neck and base is called Micmac after the Micmac people, an Algonquin group in the Canadian Maritime provinces, who were using them at the time of European contact. They are smoked by inserting a reed stem into the base. A second hole in the base is used to hang the pipe around the neck when not in use.

This "Canadischer Bauer" or Canadian Farmer was painted by Friedrich von Germann in 1778. He is smoking a Micmac pipe.
credit: Print Collection, Miriam and Ira D. Wallach Division of Art, Prints and Photographs, The New York Public Library, Astor, Lenox and Tilden Foundations

Catlinite Micmac Pipe

*"**Pierre à Calumet** . . . All the tobacco pipe heads, which the common people in Canada use, are made of this stone, and ornamented in different ways. A great part of the gentry likewise use them, especially when they are on a journey. The Indians have employed this stone for the same purposes for several ages past, and have taught it to the Europeans."*
–Peter Kalm, Swedish naturalist traveling through Quebec in 1749

This pipe shows the great influence of the Roman Catholic church on the fur trade frontier. "IHS" is the first three letters of Jesus in Greek and, along with the cross, is a common Christian symbol. The British at Michilimackinac, nominally Anglican, greatly preferred to smoke clay pipes, so this stone pipe almost certainly is French-Canadian.

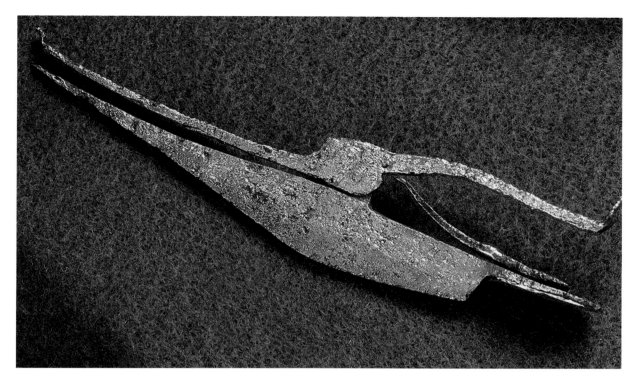

Iron Smoker's Companion

This funny-looking contraption is called a smoker's companion or fire tongs. The tongs were used to pick up a coal from the fire and hold it in a pipe bowl to light the pipe.

Here the smoker's companion is being used to light a white clay pipe, a common trade item that also was used by British residents of the fort.

Catlinite Gaming Piece

*Catlinite occurs in southwestern Minnesota and was traded across the continent. It is easily carved. This gaming piece could have been made and used by anyone at Michilimackinac — British, French, **métis** or Native American — for a board game or game of chance.*

Ivory Billiard Ball Fragment

"Upon friday the 8th febry. 1771, Ens. Johnstone...attacked William Morison, my nephew, in a most rude and Violent manner, without any evident cause, in the billiard Room."
–Daniel Morison, Surgeon's Mate, 60th Regiment, Fort Michilimackinac

Was this billiard ball used in the same room?

A variety of games can be played on a billiards table depending on the number of balls used.

Lead Whizzer

A whizzer is a disc strung on thread, twisted and looped in the manner of a cat's cradle, then pulled between the two hands to make a whizzing sound. Today they usually are made with buttons. Either children or bored soldiers may have used whizzers at Michilimackinac. Lead is easily worked; it is soft and has a low melting point. Lead balls, shot and cloth seals would have provided the raw material.

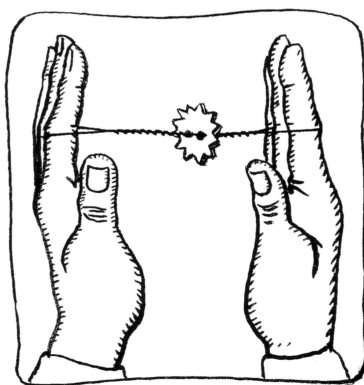

Engraved Brass Plate

At least one person at Michilimackinac did metal engraving for decoration and personalization. In addition to the letters you can see on this practice scrap, there are a "G" and an "a" on the reverse side.

Monogrammed Silver Cufflink

This silver cufflink was personalized with the initial "T." Not a very expert job, uneven and not centered, the engraving appears to have been done on the frontier.

"Jane" Brass Name Plate

Some artifacts raise more questions than they answer. Who was Jane? No Janes are listed in the Saint Anne's parish register. Women rarely appear in other records of the fort except as someone's wife or daughter, without their own first name.

Jaw Harps

"We have endeavoured to make the Winter pass as agreeably as we could, by having a Dance every week" –John Askin (Michilimackinac) to Alexander Grant (Detroit) April 28, 1778

Music was a popular way to pass the time at Michilimackinac, especially in the winter. John Askin was a fiddler. Jaw harps, which require little skill to play, were common trade goods. The upper harp is iron and the lower harp is brass.

Bone Rooster Bottle Stopper

Carving of various materials, like wood, bone or stone, was a leisure activity requiring only a knife and some raw material. It could be put to practical use as well. This rooster serves as a bottle stopper.

Knives

"1/2 Gro[ss] horn handle folding Knives"
–David McCrae accounts, Goods for one canoe for M. Landoise

Knives of all shapes and sizes were a necessity for daily life at Michilimackinac and were a popular trade item as well. Large, small, folding or sheathed, with metal, bone, horn or wood handles, traders imported hundreds each year.

Marked Iron Knife Blade

Many manufacturers stamped their name or symbol on their knife blades. These can sometimes be traced and dated. Unfortunately the mark on this blade is illegible.

Catlinite Effigy

This cute little creature is either an otter or a beaver. Its tail, which would tell us, is broken off. Catlinite beaver effigies have been found at nearby Native American sites, but they are flat and much more stylized.

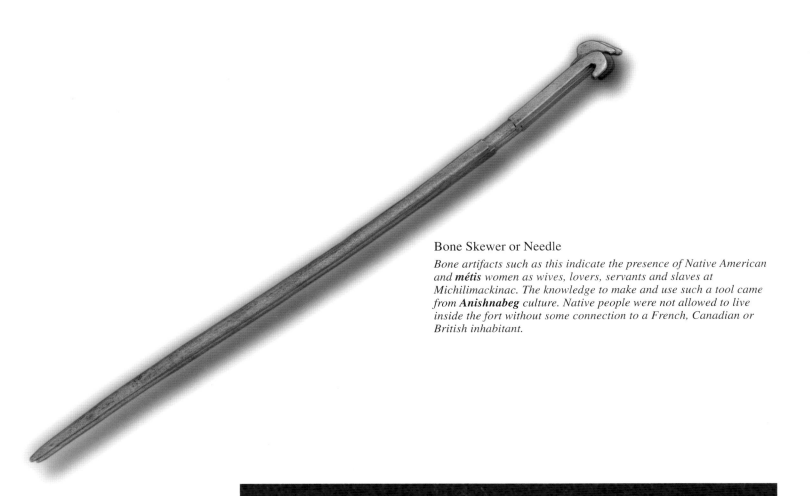

Bone Skewer or Needle

*Bone artifacts such as this indicate the presence of Native American and **métis** women as wives, lovers, servants and slaves at Michilimackinac. The knowledge to make and use such a tool came from **Anishnabeg** culture. Native people were not allowed to live inside the fort without some connection to a French, Canadian or British inhabitant.*

Native American Pot Fragment

*The **Anishnabeg** (the Odawa/ Ottawa and Ojibwa/Chippewa) and their ancestors have come to the Straits of Mackinac every summer for thousands of years to fish. Most of their fishing camps were located in protected bays, rather than on the point on which Fort Michilimackinac was built. However, pre-contact-era artifacts have been recovered over the years. This rim fragment is part of a Lake Michigan ware pot.*

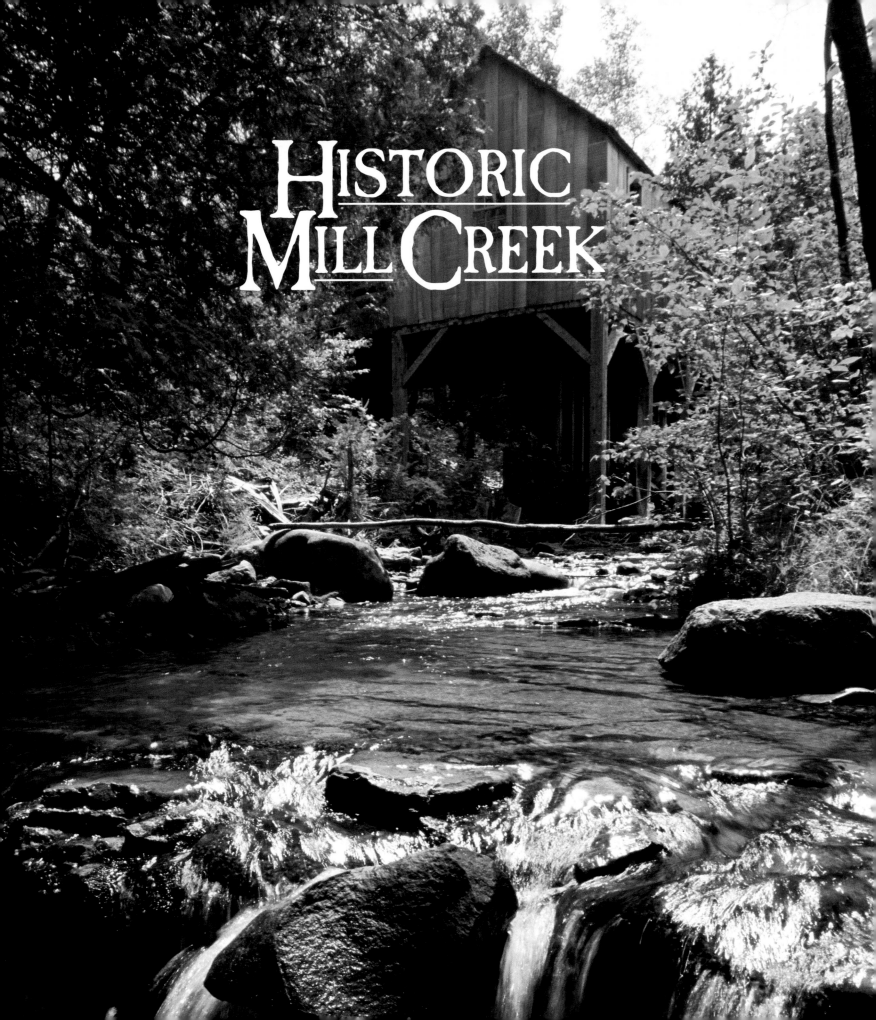

HISTORIC
MILL CREEK

American Millwright's House and Forge Hearth

The American millwright's house and forge had an unusual offset double hearth, rather than the more common H-shaped double hearth. This view, from 1975, is facing the large domestic cooking hearth. The smaller blacksmith's forge hearth is facing away from the camera.

Iron Saw-Set

"I have accordingly made a Contract for a sufficient number of boards, Which I must send to Campbell's Saw Mill for."
–Captain William Doyle, commanding officer at
Fort Mackinac, May 1793

Lumber from Campbell's saw mill was used for the construction and repair of many buildings at Fort Mackinac and the village of Mackinac Island between 1790 and 1839. A saw-set is the tool used to align the teeth of a saw at the proper angle.

A complete saw-set found at Mill Creek. Archaeologists frequently must identify artifacts from only a fragment.

Iron Horseshoe

"And the ice only closed the 22nd. Mr. Fraser had to stay at Mr. Campbell's 15 days before he got over here."
–Charles Morison (Mackinac Island) to John Askin (Detroit) February 10, 1801

With the old post of Michilimackinac abandoned, Campbell's farm and mill became the mainland jump-off point for Mackinac Island. When the lakes froze over for the winter, people rode horses or walked across the ice to the island.

Iron Harness Buckle

This large iron buckle is from a harness. Draft animals — horses and oxen — were crucial to the Mill Creek farmstead, for hauling logs to the mill, plowing fields and other agricultural purposes.

Iron Hoe Head

"whereon the said Robt. Campbell, for many years past, and until his death, did live and improve, together with the house, mills, and other improvements thereon erected and made, commonly known by the name of Campbell's farm."
–Private Claim 334, 1808

The Campbell farm included hay meadows, an orchard and a vegetable garden.

Repaired Iron Scythe Blade

"Ever since his recollection, his father, Robert Campbell occupied until his death the tract of land described in the annexed notice; that after his father's death this deponent occupied said tract until he, together with the other heirs of his said father, sold the same to Michael Dousman . . . the meadows on this tract have always been considered very valuable, and this deponent well knows that his father every year cut large quantities of hay upon them, and this deponent did the same while he was in possession of them."
–Deposition of John Campbell, age 37, in 1823 land claim

This scythe, used to harvest hay, probably was repaired at the Mill Creek site.

Iron Buckle Mold and Brass Buckle

Milling and farming required frequent repairs to tools, such as the scythe blade pictured previously, so blacksmithing and other metal work was always part of life at Mill Creek. During the Campbell era metal work took place in the workshop. A forge took up one room of the American Millwright's House. This buckle mold dates to the Campbell era. Only one half is shown, although both halves were recovered.

Bone Powder Measure

Although the Mill Creek settlement was closely connected to Mackinac Island, the Straits were not always passable due to weather. The entire Straits of Mackinac region was isolated from the rest of the world in the winter months until the coming of the railroad and icebreakers in the late nineteenth century. The families living at Mill Creek had to be fairly self-reliant. One of the Campbells probably carved this bone gunpowder measure.

Iron Saw Dog Fragment

"Michael Dousman had a saw-mil about two miles distant from our logs and we soon had them there."
–Martin Heydenburk, builder of Mission Church, Mackinac Island, 1830

Saw dogs are used to hold logs in place on the sawmill carriage while they are being sawn.

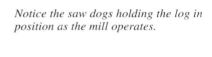

Notice the saw dogs holding the log in position as the mill operates.

Iron Padlock

This padlock is amazingly well preserved. The flap protecting the keyhole from the weather still moves. The generally sandy soil in the Straits region drains well, which leads to good preservation of most artifacts. Dry artifacts corrode more slowly than damp ones. The cold winter temperatures and frozen ground slow down many decay processes.

American Military Buttons

A variety of military buttons have been found at Mill Creek. Soldiers picking up lumber at the mill may have lost them. Another possibility is that the millwright may have been a former soldier who continued wearing uniform parts while working. Wayne's Legion, the first American soldiers at Fort Mackinac, arriving in 1796, wore the top button, known as the frog-legged eagle. The script "I" was issued to the infantry from 1812 to 1815. There were no United States infantry stationed at Fort Mackinac from 1805 until its capture in 1812, only artillery. The first American soldiers to return to the fort in 1815 wore this button. The Corps of Artillery used the eagle on the cannon button from 1814 to 1821.

Private, 10th Royal Veteran Battalion

Royal Veteran Battalion Brass Hat Plate

This hat plate was among the first artifacts found by the three local historians who brought the Mill Creek site to the Mackinac Island State Park Commission's attention. The design includes many British symbols, including "GR" (Latin initials for King George), the crown, lion, flags and motto of the Order of the Garter. The British infantry used this hat plate design from 1800 to 1813. This particular plate probably came from a soldier of the 10th Royal Veteran Battalion, the unit that captured Fort Mackinac at the beginning of the War of 1812.

Iron Knife with Brass Handle

Knives were as important to daily life at Mill Creek as they had been at Michilimackinac. This knife, found at the Campbell house, has a nearly identical handle to one found at Michilimackinac.

Iron Fork with Bone Handle

Although four-tined forks were developed for fine dining in the mid-eighteenth century, two-tined forks continued to be used long afterward in informal settings. This fork has a hand carved bone handle.

Nickel-Plated Spoon

Some items have not changed much in the past two hundred years. Cleaned up, this nickel-plated spoon would look right at home in a modern American kitchen.

Colorful Ceramics

The Industrial Revolution led to an explosion of new technologies in the ceramics industry. Many colors and patterns became widely available at affordable prices. Banded ceramics were particularly popular in the first half of the nineteenth century.

Small Bottle

Bottle function is extremely difficult to determine based on form. A small bottle such as this could have held condiments, pharmaceutical or toilet items. Once emptied of their original contents, bottles were reused until they broke.

Transfer-Printed Cup

Transfer printing allowed intricate designs to be mass-produced. Blue was the most popular color, but black, brown, green, red and purple transfer-printed wares were all produced.

Early nineteenth-century households used a variety of ceramic types at the same time. This table setting from the Biddle House on Mackinac Island would be equally correct in the American Millwright's House at Mill Creek.

Ceramic Maker's Mark

Maker's marks became increasingly common throughout the nineteenth century. Finding fragments of them helps identify what the pattern looked like and where and when it was made. This mark is from a "Park Scenery" plate manufactured by George Phillips of Longport, Staffordshire between 1834 and 1848.

Marked Button

*Buttons are sometimes stamped with a maker's mark. This plain-faced copper alloy button is stamped "LONDON*IMPERIAL," a mark we have not yet been able to trace.*

Brass Wedding Ring

The two entwined hearts engraved on this ring suggest that it is a wedding band. It was found near a floor joist in the American Millwright's House. How did it get there? Did someone search for it? Was the owner sorry it was lost?

Decorated Mother-of-Pearl Buttons

These small mother-of-pearl buttons suggest that a woman lived at the American Millwright's House. Most of the artifacts found at the house were items related to daily subsistence that could have been used by anyone, rather than personal items.

Hibernia/Wellington Coin

Ireland issued this copper coin to commemorate Wellington's triumphant return from India in 1805. One side has a harp and crown, with the word HIBERNIA and the date 1805. The other side has a man's profile and the words FIELD MARSHAL WELLINGTON. Even more intriguing is where the coin was found, under the floor near the north door of the American Millwright's House. Irish American traditions include the custom of placing a copper under the floor, near the door of a new house for good luck. Was the American Millwright an Irish American?

Pierced Coin

This 1836 copper U.S. coin has had holes drilled in it, possibly for use as jewelry or other ornament. Based on its size and composition, it appears to be a one-cent piece, but the coin has been so badly scratched that the center designs are illegible.

Brass Bell

This bell is a mystery artifact. Not in what it is, but in what it was used for. It is the wrong shape and size to be used on livestock. Was it a dinner bell? A door bell?

BIDDLE HOUSE
Mackinac Island

Feather Edge Plate

Edged plates were common in the early nineteenth century. Blue was the most common edge color, although green is sometimes seen. The pattern could be feathered, scalloped or a plain line. This plate is from a privy at the Biddle House. The ceramics and other items used to fill in the privy are contemporary with the American occupation at Mill Creek.

Castle Pattern Plate

This plate shows the Castle pattern developed by Josiah Spode based on the prints "The Gate of Sebastian" and "Ponte Molle." The pattern was pirated by other manufacturers, including James and Ralph Clews of Cobridge, Staffordshire, who made this plate. The back is stamped with their mark: CLEWS WARRANTED STAFFORDSHIRE stamped around a crown. This plate was produced between 1815 and 1834.

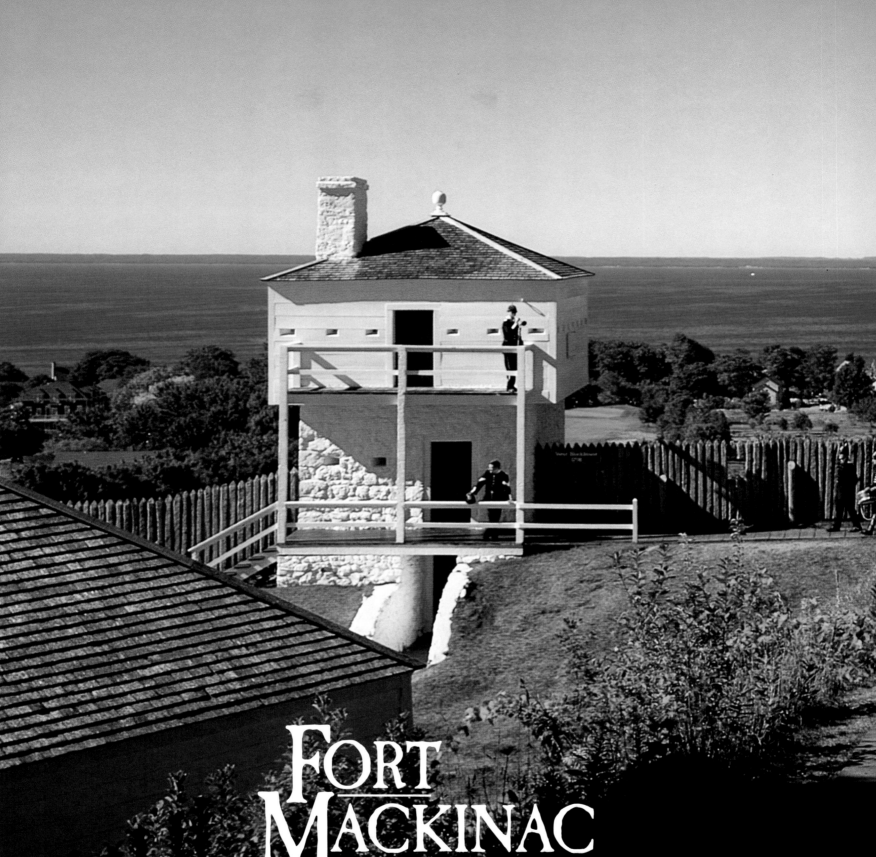

FORT MACKINAC

British Well

"It would likewise be very important that a deep well formerly cut through a rock inside the Fort and which has been allowed to fill up by the sides falling in should be cleared . . . "
–Captain Richard Bullock (Mackinac) to Military Secretary Noah Freer (Montreal) October 23, 1813.

An eighty-foot deep well was one of the original components of Fort Mackinac. It was completely filled, rather than repaired, following the War of 1812. A portion of the casing, shown here during excavation in 1981, is visible through a viewing port today.

George III Half-Penny

This 1776 George III halfpenny actually predates Fort Mackinac. It was found during the restoration of the fort wall. One of the soldiers who helped build the fort between 1779 and 1781 probably dropped it.

Royal Regiment of Artillery Button

A few men from the Royal Regiment of Artillery were stationed at Fort Mackinac during the entire early British period (1779-1796). This gilt officer's button from that regiment belonged to Lieutenant Christopher Meyers, the only commissioned officer from that regiment to serve at Fort Mackinac.

Iron Architectural Bracket

The provision storehouse was one of the buildings moved from Fort Michilimackinac to Fort Mackinac, where it was located behind and under the 1828 post hospital. Its location was excavated at both forts, making it one of the few buildings anywhere to be excavated twice! This iron architectural bracket dates to the initial British 1780-1796 occupation of Fort Mackinac.

The provision storehouse building served many uses before it was torn down due to its poor condition. This drawing shows the hospital built on the storehouse foundation in 1827. The log building to the right is part of the original provision storehouse moved from Michilimackinac and serving as a sutler's store in 1827. Both buildings burned to the ground October 31, 1827.
Image courtesy of Clements Library, University of Michigan

Early American Hat Cockade

An artilleryman at Fort Mackinac between 1802 and 1808 wore this leather cockade with brass eagle. Workmen restoring the East Blockhouse in 1967 found it on top of a ceiling beam. Many artifacts have been found while restoring buildings on Mackinac Island. These have helped to date and interpret the structures.

Lietenant, Artillerists and Engineers

ERIC MANDERS

Clay Pipes

White clay pipes are commonly found at British and American sites dating from the eighteenth to mid-nineteenth century. We find them at both mainland and island sites in the straits area. These two bowls are from a cache found under the Quartermaster's Storehouse at Fort Mackinac. The initials "T.D." are a common design; here they are surrounded by thirteen stars, probably representing the original thirteen colonies. The thistle design bowl has a rose on the other side.

Iron Scissors

Scissors are frequently associated with cutting cloth prior to sewing, and so were a common item in the fur trade along with textiles. This particular pair was found in an early American (1796-1812) layer of the Provision Storehouse. They may have been for trade or for use by military tailors.

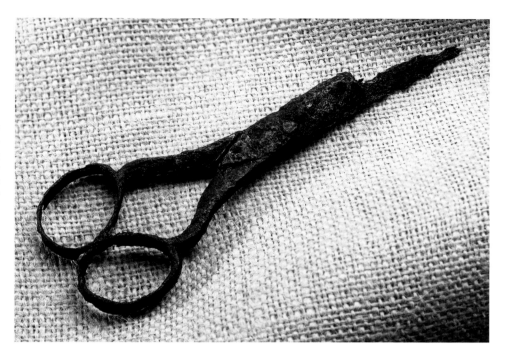

East Blockhouse Buttons

The foundation of the east blockhouse was repaired during the recent restoration of the Fort Mackinac wall and other masonry work at the fort. Numerous buttons were found around the edge of the blockhouse. They may have been swept out through trapdoors in the overhanging second floor. The Americans constructed the blockhouse after their arrival in 1796 and used it as a barracks as well as a defensive structure. The buttons shown here are some of the more unusual found. All date to the early nineteenth century. The buttons numbered 6 and 16 with UNITED STATES around them are infantry buttons issued from 1798 to 1802. Although only the 1st regiment served at Fort Mackinac, buttons from nine regiments have been found here. The army anticipated higher enlistments than they got, so they had surplus buttons which were distributed regardless of regiment. Note that the UNITED STATES on the 16th button reads from right to left, instead of the usual left to right. The script "LA," for Light Artillery, button is another surplus button from a unit that never served at Mackinac. The script "RA" button is from the 2nd Regiment of Artillery. Men from this unit were stationed at Fort Mackinac from 1796 to 1812. This particular button was manufactured from 1810 to 1813. The eagle with "R" shield on his chest is from the Regiment of Riflemen. This button was manufactured from 1812 to 1814. Soldiers from this unit were among the first American troops to return to Fort Mackinac after the War of 1812. The button with the anchor is from a naval uniform. American and British navy buttons from the early nineteenth century are difficult to tell apart. A few sailors from the Royal Navy were at Fort Mackinac during the War of 1812.

Brass British Hat Plate

This hat plate fragment is from a "Belgic" shako, first issued to British troops in 1811. This equipment did not arrive at Mackinac until the autumn of 1813. This style of hat was worn by men from the 1st Regiment of Foot, Michigan Fencibles, Royal Newfoundland Fencible Infantry and Corps of Royal Engineers, all stationed at Fort Mackinac during the waning months of the War of 1812.

This young man, portraying an ensign in the Regiment de Meuron, is about to participate in a re-enactment of the 1814 Battle for Mackinac Island. Notice the hat plate.

Brass United States Infantry Hat Plate

This is the lower half of a plate that would have gone on the front of an American infantryman's hat from 1814 to 1821. The design, though difficult to make out, is of a flag, drum and shield. The missing portion shows an eagle above clouds.

Shoe Parts:
leather sole and cleat, iron boot heel plate

Following the War of 1812 the rooms of the provision storehouse building were used for a variety of other purposes. In 1816 one of these was housing tailors and shoemakers of the 3rd infantry. These shoe parts are remnants of the shoemakers' and tailors' activities. They were found with other leather shoe heels, shoe soles, fragments of leather, iron boot heel cleats, bits of cloth, felt and buttons.

Bone Button Blank

This piece of bone is scrap from the making of bone button backs. A circular drill was used to cut bone discs from flat pieces of animal bone. These bone discs were used as backs in multi-part buttons or alone as plain buttons. This piece of bone scrap is further evidence of the post-1812 tailors' activities.

Hand-Painted Pearlware Pitcher

Pearlware was a common type of ceramic in the early nineteenth century. Even after transfer printing was developed, hand-painted designs continued, and were somewhat cheaper. This reassembled pitcher is one of the most complete vessels found at Fort Mackinac because most large trash was disposed of outside the fort walls.

Microscope Lens

Part of the provision storehouse was used as the post hospital from about 1815 until it was razed and rebuilt in 1827. This objective lens from a microscope was used by one of the physicians who served during that time. The most famous was Dr. William Beaumont. Beaumont began his groundbreaking observations of human digestion here in 1822, when Alexis St. Martin, a voyageur, was accidentally shot in the stomach at close range. Although Beaumont saved St. Martin's life, the wound never entirely closed and Beaumont was able to use the opening to perform digestive experiments. Unfortunately this lens was found in an undateable mixed context.

William Beaumont served at Fort Mackinac from 1820 to 1825. This 1832 painting shows him with his wife Deborah and children Lucretia, Sarah and Israel.

Image courtesy of University of Chicago

Bone Knife

This little knife is carved entirely from bone, including the blades. Someone must have spent many hours crafting this as a showpiece or gift. It has no practical function.

Ink Bottle

Ink bottles are common in trash pits outside Fort Mackinac. Cone shaped bottles like this are the most common and usually date to the nineteenth century. The bottom of this bottle is embossed "CARTER'S." The Carter's Ink Company was founded in Boston in 1858 and continues to make stamp pads and ink-related office products to this day. Separately bottled ink became rare after the invention of the ballpoint pen in the 1930s.

Coffee Mill Plate

"J. & E. PARKER'S UNION MILL Pat. Nov. 20, 1855 & Feb. 7, 1860"

The Parker family, Charles, John and Edmund were prolific makers of coffee mills and other domestic hardware from the 1830s to the 1890s. The firm was based in Meriden, Connecticut. This brass identification plate was found in the Fort Mackinac blacksmith shop. Was it for the blacksmith's use at the shop or was he repairing this iron mill for someone?

This is what the coffee mill looked like.
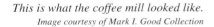
Image courtesy of Mark I. Good Collection

Champagne Bottle

A stone-lined well in excess of eighty feet deep was one of the original features of Fort Mackinac. It failed prior to 1812 and was filled in over the next 170 years. The demolition of the adjacent original powder magazine in 1878 led to additional trash deposits. Because they needed to fill a large hole, soldiers discarded large pieces of refuse that normally would have gone in a dump outside the fort walls. This intact champagne bottle was excavated from the well in 1981. Part of its paper label is still visible.

General Service Button

In 1854 the American army finally settled on a standard button design for all enlisted men. This design, an eagle with a lined shield, was used with minor variations until 1902. This particular button is marked HORSTMAN BROS & CO/PHILA. The acidic soil of the blacksmith shop corroded the brass in this button.

Brass Helmet Spike and Base

The United State Army ordered a major re-design of its uniforms in 1872. Because the Prussian and British armies were the most successful in the world at that time, the Americans copied some elements from them. This trend became even more pronounced in 1881 when the army adopted a spiked helmet for all foot troops. The spike base has an oak leaf design.

Costumed interpreters at Fort Mackinac portray men of the 23rd Regiment of Infantry, the second-to-last regiment to serve there. Notice the spike and base on the helmets.

Duffy's Malt Whiskey Bottle

Q: What kind of liquor was taken in the cell by said prisoner?

A: Duffy's Malt Whiskey

In November 1888, Private Frank Darlington, company K, 23rd infantry, was court martialled for assisting in the procurement of liquor for prisoners confined in the Fort Mackinac Post Guard House with him. Private Darlington was confined in the guard house at the time for being absent without leave six times in the preceding 14 months! He was found guilty on the liquor charge and dishonorably discharged. This bottle was excavated from the Custer Road dump behind Fort Mackinac.

Fort Mackinac courts martial from the 1880s are re-enacted daily during the summer months.

U.S.Q.M.D. Plate

This plain white plate is mainly of interest due to the initials stamped on the back. U.S.Q.M.D. stands for United States Quartermaster Department. The Trenton China Company, of Trenton, New Jersey, supplied plates like this to the army from 1870 until 1897. This plate was found at a dump behind Fort Mackinac along with matching bowls and serving pieces.

U.S.Q.M.D. Tumblers

These Quartermaster Department tumblers were excavated from the same dump as the plate. They were originally clear. Manganese was added to glass as a de-coloring agent from the mid-1880s until about World War I. It takes on an amethyst color when exposed to the sun. The tumblers have fourteen facets around the bottom. Octagonal beer mugs with the same mark were found as well. Non-military trash from the soldiers and their wives and children was disposed of in the same location.

National Park Drug Store Bottle

This pharmaceutical bottle was manufactured for the NATIONAL PARK DRUG STORE, DR J R BAILEY & SON, MACKINAC ISLAND MICH. The Bailey family ran a pharmacy and general store for about seventy years on Mackinac Island. Dr. John R. Bailey served at Fort Mackinac. His son was Matthew Gray Bailey. Mackinac Island was the nation's second national park from 1875 to 1895.

*This advertisement ran in the 1909 edition of **Mackinac, formerly Michilimackinac**, a guidebook to Mackinac Island by John Read Bailey, M.D.*

JOHN R. BAILEY, M. D.
Late Post Surgeon, Fort Mackinac

MATTHEW G. BAILEY
Pharmacist

ESTABLISHED 1854

National Park
Drug Store

OLDEST DRUG HOUSE IN THE NORTHWEST

John R. Bailey & Son

Mackinac Island, Mich.

Drugs, Medicines, Wines and Liquors,
Fine Perfumes, Toilet Articles,
Fancy Goods, Druggists'
Sundries,
Fancy Groceries, Glassware, Hardware,
General Merchandise, Sporting
Goods, Fishing Tackle,
Confectionery,
Cigars, Tobacco, Paints, Oils, Wall Paper,
Stationery, Optical Goods.

HEADQUARTERS FOR
"MACKINAC, FORMERLY MICHILIMACKINAC"
By JOHN R. BAILEY, M. D., Etc.
Sold by Agents Generally

PHYSICIANS' PRESCRIPTIONS A SPECIALTY

GRADUATES IN PHARMACY IN CHARGE

ICE CREAM SODA

GINGER ALE, SHERBET AND MINERAL WATERS ON DRAUGHT

1895 Penny

On September 16, 1895 the U.S. army marched out of Fort Mackinac for the last time. The fort, military reservation and Mackinac Island National Park were turned over to the State of Michigan and the Mackinac Island State Park Commission. One hundred years later, during the commission's centennial summer, this 1895 copper penny was excavated at the site of the former blacksmith shop within Fort Mackinac.

"DEUX LOUTRE" Lead Token

Archaeology often leads to more questions than answers. This token, found during the Fort Mackinac wall restoration, is a recent example of this. "DEUX LOUTRE" means two otters in French. Was this a fur trade token? Is 1607 a date? A transaction number? Is the squiggle at the bottom a Native American symbol? Nothing else like this is known from the region.

SOURCES FOR HISTORIC QUOTATIONS

Powder Magazine — Gérin-Lajoie 1976:6

Solomon-Levy-Parant House — Fortier n.d.:21-22

Creamware Platter — Askin 1776

Whitefish Skeleton — Henry 1809:54-55

Buttons — Wallace 1934:51

Brass Thimble — Quaife 1928:132

Iron Awl with Bone Handle — McCrae 1777-1787

Glass Necklace Beads — McCrae 1777-1787

Brass Hawk Bell — Henry 1809:24

Brass Finger Rings — McCrae 1777-1787

Limestone Micmac Pipe — Henry 1809:24

Catlinite Micmac Pipe — Kalm 1987:498

Ivory Billiard Ball Fragment — May 1960:26

Jaw Harps — Quaife 1928:77

Knives — McCrae 1777-1787

Iron Saw-Set — Michigan Pioneer and Historical Society 1888:48

Iron Horseshoe — Thwaites 1910:294

Iron Hoe Head — Lowrie 1832a:408

Repaired Iron Scythe Blade — Lowrie 1832b:222-223

Iron Saw Dog Fragment — Michigan Pioneer and Historical Society 1903:22

British Well — Michigan Pioneer and Historical Society 1909:424

Duffy's Malt Whiskey Bottle — Judge Advocate General 1888

APPENDIX I:
Artifact Catalog Information

Artifact	Catalog Number	Reference	Dimensions
Powder Magazine		Heldman & Minnerly 1977	
Solomon-Levy Root Cellar		Halchin 1985 Heldman 1986	
French Faience Plate		Miller & Stone 1970	8 1/4" diameter
English Delft Bowl		Miller & Stone 1970	6 7/8" top diameter 2 7/8" high
Chinese Export Porcelain Saucer	MS2.2253.15	Miller & Stone 1970	6 1/8" diameter
Creamware Cup	MS2.2865 MS2.2869.6 MS2.3004.20	Miller & Stone 1970	2 5/8" high 1 3/4" base diameter
Creamware Platter		Miller & Stone 1970	18 3/4" wide
Whieldon-type Teacup	MS2.294.29 MS2.538.14	Maxwell & Binford 1961 Miller & Stone 1970	1 17/32" high
English Red Stoneware Teapot	MS2.2253	Miller & Stone 1970	4 1/8" base diameter 3 9/16" high
Green Glazed Earthenware Bowl	MS2.2080.11	Miller & Stone 1970	4 3/4" base diameter 8 13/16" top interior diameter
British Case Bottle	MS2.2891.11 et al	Brown 1971	9 31/32" high 3 1/4" base 47 oz. capacity
French Case Bottle	MS2.4076.2	Brown 1971	8 3/8" high 2 31/32" base maximum 24 oz. capacity
British Wine Bottle	MS2.4627.8	Brown 1971	8 5/32" high 3 3/4" base 26 oz.
Turlington Bottle	MS2.2704.2	Brown 1971	3 11/16" high
Molded Glass Tankard	MS2.2892.5	Brown 1971	3 1/2" base 6 3/16" current height

Artifact	Catalog Number	Reference	Dimensions
Engraved Cordial Glass	MS2.2704.3	Brown 1971	4 5/16" high 2 3/8" base diameter
Cast Iron Pot	MS2.1.0.115	Stone 1974	9 1/2" high 7/32" thick
Whitefish Skeleton	MS2.10451.11	Scott 1985 Scott 1991	17" long
Bone Harpoon	MS2.11028.39	Stone 1974 Morand 1994	4 21/32" long 5/8" base width
Chicken Egg	MS2.7358.18	Scott 1985 Scott 1991	2 7/16" long
Red Earthenware Chamber Pot	MS2.4580.2	Miller & Stone 1970	5 1/16" high
Bone Comb	MS2.1416.11	Stone 1974	1 13/16" long 1 13/16" base width 1 21/32" top width 1/16" thick
Bone Syringe	MS2.6143.1		2 11/16" long 13/32" barrel diameter
Plain 8th Button	MS2.5755.1	Stone 1974 Dunnigan 1975	3/4" diameter
Horse 8th Button	MS2.11410.23	Stone 1974 Dunnigan 1975 Evans 2001	11/16" diameter
Checked 8th Button	MS2.2007.5	Stone 1974 Dunnigan 1975	7/8" diameter
Plain 10th Button	MS2.1244.20	Stone 1974 Dunnigan 1975	15/16" diameter
Silver-plated 10th Button	MS2.2457.6	Stone 1974 Dunnigan 1975	15/16" diameter
60th Button	MS2.2781.4	Stone 1974 Dunnigan 1975	15/16" diameter
18th Regiment Button	MS2.1224.1	Dunnigan 1975 Steven Baule 1999 (pers. comm.)	21/32" diameter
Iron Flintlock Lockplate and Cock	MS2.3026.2 MS2.2980.3	Hamilton 1976	6 3/8" total length
Brass Flintlock Sideplate	MS2.4204.2	Hamilton 1976	5 15/16" long

Artifact	Catalog Number	Reference	Dimensions
Crown/Shield/Face Brass Flintlock Escutcheon	MS2.885.9	Hamilton 1976	1 25/32" long
Bust Brass Flintlock Escutcheon	MS2.2499.11	Hamilton 1976	1 11/16" long
Brass Flintlock Buttplate Finial	MS2.722.5	Hamilton 1976	1 5/16" long
Brass Flintlock Triggerguard Finial	MS2.12718.17	Hamilton 1976	7/8" long
Iron Door Handle/Latch	MS2.1	Morand 1994	10" current length 2 7/8" maximum width
Window Pane	MS2.3345.1	Brown 1971	7 1/2" x 8 1/2"
Iron Lock	MS2.1.0.116	Stone 1974	3" high 3 1/16" wide
Iron Keyhole Escutcheon	MS2.3284.3	Stone 1974	3 13/16" long keyhole section is 7/8" wide
Iron Key	MS2.6703.33	Stuart 1959	6 3/32" long
Brass Barrel Band	MS2.1347.6	Neumann & Kravic 1975	Irregular — approx. 2 7/8" x 7/8"
Wax Seal	MS2.5034		15/16" present top-bottom diameter
Intaglio Letter Seal	MS2.4893.5		1 3/8" total height 19/32" intaglio diameter 5/8" intaglio thickness
Intaglio Letter Seal	MS2.11441.36	Evans 2001	1 1/8" high intaglio 1/2" x 15/32"
Penknife	MS2.69.6	Stone 1974	2 1/8" long
Iron Telescope	MS2.1556.10	Stone 1974	8 1/4" present combined length 15/16" eyepiece diameter 1 3/16" objective end diameter
Bone Sundial Base	MS2.2846.3	Stone 1974	2" long 1 9/16" wide 3/8" thick
Coin: George I Halfpenny		Heldman 1980	1 1/16" diameter 1/16" thick
Coin: Louis XV Two Sou		Heldman 1980	7/8" diameter 1/32" thick

Artifact	Catalog Number	Reference	Dimensions
Coin: Philip V Medio Real	MS2.4607	Heldman 1980	9/16" diameter 1/32" thick
Coin: Two Bit Piece	MS2.5034.17	Heldman 1980	25/32" maximum radius 1/16" thick
Brass Spigot	MS2.5400.3	Stone 1974	4 9/16" total present length
Textile Fragment	MS2.4761.7	Stone 1974	3 1/2" long 1 1/16" wide
Rooster Lead Seal	MS2.2247.2	Stone 1974 Adams 1989	3/4" diameter
Crocodile Lead Seal	MS2.12805.9	Stone 1974 Adams 1989	20/32" diameter
CDI Lead Seal	MS2.11396.26	Stone 1974 Adams 1989	21/32" x 21/32" x 23/32" (base)
Plain Brass Buckle	MS2.657.3	Stone 1974	1 1/16" x 25/32" (frame)
Tracery Brass Buckle	MS2.4644.2	Stone 1974	1 29/32" x 1 15/32"
Ornate Brass Buckle Fragment	MS2.694.2	Stone 1974	1 13/16" x 1 1/4" (existing frame)
Beaded Brass Buckle	MS2.1003.2	Stone 1974	1 1/2" x 1 3/16"
Silver Gilt Swirl Button (CIISAT5Vp)	MS2.4862.11	Stone 1974	29/32" diameter
Silver Star Button	MS2.2687.11	Stone 1974	11/16" diameter
Brass Checked Button	MS2.6749.49	Stone 1974	19/32" diameter
Brass Floral Button Crown	MS2.5410.40	Stone 1974	19/32" diameter
Brass Starburst Button	MS2.4735.7	Stone 1974	5/8" diameter
Brass Thimble	MS2.5429.6	Stone 1974	11/16" base diameter 1/2" top diameter 25/32" high
Iron Awl with Bone Handle	MS2.4880.2	Stone 1974	4 1/2" total length
Faceted Turquoise Necklace Bead (CIISAT3Vb)	MS2.8765.38	Stone 1974	5/8" long 13/32" diameter
Twisted Red Necklace Bead (CISAT8Va)	MS2.9390.4	Stone 1974	1 1/2" long 5/16" diameter
Convex White Necklace Bead w/red & blue stripes (CISCT1Va)	MS2.8474.4	Stone 1974	17/32" long 9/32" diameter

Artifact	Catalog Number	Reference	Dimensions
Round Blue-green Necklace Bead w/white stripes (CISCT5Vb)	MS2.10333.2	Stone 1974	3/16" diameter through hole
Man-in-the-Moon Bead (CIISAT5Va)	MS2.290	Maxwell & Binford 1961 Stone 1974 Lorenzini & Karklins 2000/01	11/16" diameter 7/32" thick
Brass Hawk Bell	MS2.715.1	Stone 1974	13/16" diameter
Silver Earring	MS2.11153.44	Stone 1974	1 13/32" long 1/4" ball diameter
Brass Jesuit Ring — round w/heart	MS2.58.9	Cleland 1972 Stone 1974 Hauser 1982	12/32" x 13/32"
Brass Jesuit Ring — octagonal w/LV	MS2.1217.2	Cleland 1972 Stone 1974 Hauser 1982	9/16" x 9/16"
Brass Jesuit Ring — heart w/IXXI	MS2.1655.19	Cleland 1972 Stone 1974 Hauser 1982	3/8" broadest point across
Brass St. Ignatius Medallion	MS2.1	Rinehart 1990 Jim Boynton, S.J. 2002 (pers. comm.)	29/32" high (not including loop) 13/16" wide
Brass Crucifix	MS2.2022.3	Stone 1974 Rinehart 1990	1 11/16" long 1 1/8" wide
Rosary	MS2.12767.8		1/4" sm. bead diameter convex beads vary
Clay Medallion	MS2.11664.25	Evans 2001	1 3/32" wide
Plain Finger Brass Ring	MS2.2588.02	Stone 1974	5/32" band width 5/8" outside diameter 9/16" inside diameter
Brass Finger Ring w/green & blue sets	MS2.3873.1	Stone 1974	3/4" outside diameter 11/16" inside diameter
Brass Finger Ring w/clear & blue sets	MS2.8916.17	Stone 1974	7/8" outside diameter 13/16" inside diameter
Brass Earring	MS2.6744.55	Stone 1974	15/16" front length
Brass Cufflink	MS2.1196.6	Stone 1974	7/16" diameter
Repaired Cufflink	MS2.120.4	Morand 1994	13/32" cufflink diameter 7/16" hawk bell diameter

Artifact	Catalog Number	Reference	Dimensions
Limestone Micmac Pipe	MS2.2153.4 MS2.2273	Hauser 1983 Morand 1994	1 27/32" high 3 1/32" base length 3/4" top bowl diameter
Catlinite Micmac Pipe	MS2.11448.2	Evans 2001	1 5/8" high 1" long
Iron Smoker's Companion	MS2.2308.2	Stone 1974	4 13/16" total length
Catlinite Gaming Piece	MS2.12096.27	Evans 2001	21/32" diameter
Ivory Billiard Ball Fragment	MS2.11834.25		2 1/16" present diameter
Lead Whizzer	MS2.2356.2	Stone 1974 Morand 1994	1 3/8" point to point diameter
Engraved Brass Plate	MS2.5109.3		1 7/16" widest point
Monogrammed Silver Cufflink	MS2.751.4	Stone 1974	11/16" x 11/16"
"Jane" Brass Name Plate	MS2.4266.1		Irregular — approx. 1 7/8" x1 3/16"
Iron Jaw Harp	MS2.91.1	Maxwell & Binford 1961 Stone 1974	2 7/32" long 1 1/8" wide 1 5/8" tongue length
Brass Jaw Harp	MS2.10745.11	Stone 1974	2 3/32" long 15/16" wide
Bone Rooster Bottle Stopper	MS2.4945.4		2 1/32" high
Bone Handled Clasp Knife	MS2.2815.3	Stone 1974	3 7/16" long closed
Iron Handled Clasp Knife	MS2.1091.2	Stone 1974	4 1/2" long closed
Marked Iron Knife Blade	MS2.883.2	Stone 1974	6 1/8" long
Catlinite Effigy	MS2.6702.25	Cleland 1971 Heldman 1977	1 27/32" long 3/4" high
Bone Skewer/Needle	MS2.10922.19	Morand 1994	8 11/16" long
Native American Pot Fragment	MS2.11874.1	Maxwell 1964 Evans 2001	6 1/4" present rim circumference
American Millwright's House Fireplace		Martin 1985 Kempton 1986 Scott 1994	
Iron Saw-Set	20CN8.234.5	Martin 1985	Irregular — 1 5/8" maximum current width
Iron Horseshoe	20CN8.25.80	Martin 1985	7 1/4" long 5 27/32" wide

Artifact	Catalog Number	Reference	Dimensions
Iron Harness Buckle	20CN8.283.4	Martin 1985	2 1/2" x 1 5/8" (not including tongue)
Iron Hoe Head	20CN8.226.17	Martin 1985	7 1/16" long 4 1/2" wide
Repaired Iron Scythe Blade	20CN8.330.2	Martin 1985	9 1/4" long 2 1/4" base width
Iron Buckle Mold	20CN8.47.11	Martin 1985	29/32" x 7/8" (buckle dimension)
Brass Buckle	20CN8.25	Martin 1985	1 1/8" x 29/32"
Bone Powder Measure	20CN8.357.2	Martin 1985	2 7/8" long 13/16" maximum diameter (irregular)
Iron Saw Dog Fragment	20CN8.3618.18		11" total length
Iron Padlock	20CN8.376.2	Martin 1985	4 23/32" total current open length 1" thick
American Script I Button	20CN8.153.6	Campbell 1965 Dunnigan 1975 Martin 1985 Kempton 1986	3/4" diameter
American Frog-Leg Eagle Button	20CN8.117.4	Campbell 1965 Martin 1985 Kempton 1986	7/8" diameter
American Artillery CORPS Button	20CN8.247.6	Campbell 1965 Martin 1985 Kempton 1986	3/4" diameter
Royal Veteran Battalion Brass Hat Plate	1995.1.362	Dunnigan 1975 Martin 1985	6 1/8" x 4 1/8"
Iron Knife with Brass Handle	20CN8.219.3	Martin 1985	6" present length
Iron Fork with Bone Handle	20CN8.3378.53		6 7/8" total length irregular handle diameter
Nickel-Plated Spoon	20CN8.301.3		5 29/32" long
Polychrome Hand-Painted Pearlware Fragment	20CN8.1154A.3 et al	Martin 1985 Kempton 1986 Scott 1994	4 7/8" present circumference

Artifact	Catalog Number	Reference	Dimensions
Red & Green Transfer-Printed Whiteware Fragment	20CN8.1350A.6 20CN8.1422A	Martin 1985 Kempton 1986 Scott 1994	3 3/8" present circumference
Marbled Annular Pearlware Fragment	20CN8.1303A 20CN8.1354A	Martin 1985 Kempton 1986	3 1/8" height of straight bowl section
Small Bottle	20CN8.385.2 et al	Martin 1985	6 9/16" high 1 7/8" base diameter
Transfer-Printed Cup	20CN8.3336.1	Martin 1985 Kempton 1986 Scott 1994	2 3/8" base diameter
Ceramic Maker's Mark	20CN8.302A(C)112 20CN8.302A(0)127	Coysh & Henrywood 1982 Martin 1985 Kempton 1986 Scott 1994	Irregular — 1 1/2" current maximum dimension
Marked Button	20CN8.312.2	Martin 1985 Kempton 1986	11/16" diameter
Brass Wedding Ring	20CN8.2747.5	Scott 1994	13/16" outside diameter 25/32" inside diameter tapered band
Mother-of-Pearl Button	20CN8.1767.37	Scott 1994	3/8" diameter
Mother-of-Pearl Button	20CN8.1769.14	Scott 1994	3/8" diameter
Mother-of-Pearl Button	20CN8.392.2	Scott 1994	3/8" diameter
Hibernia/Wellington Coin	20CN8.2748.3	Scott 1994	1 1/8" diameter 1/16" thick
Pierced Coin	20CN8.3325.33		1 1/4" diameter 1/16" thick
Brass Bell	20CN8.1049A.6		2 17/32" tall 2 7/32" base diameter
Feather Edge Plate	MS5.3.1	Stone 1975	6" diameter
Castle Pattern Plate	MS5.5.1	Stone 1975 Coysh & Henrywood 1982	10" diameter
British Well		Wright 1985	
George III Half-Penny	FMW.680	Branstner & Branstner 2002	1 1/8" diameter 1/16" thick
Royal Regiment of Artillery Button	MS3.C1P14.28	Dunnigan 1973 Grange 1987	11/16" diameter

Artifact	Catalog Number	Reference	Dimensions
Iron Architectural Bracket	MS3.C1H88.21	Grange 1987	4 11/16" wide 4 1/32" long
Early American Hat Cockade		Dunnigan 1975 Emerson 1996	4" diameter
T.D. Star Clay Pipe		Petersen 1963	27/32" widest diameter
Thistle & Rose Clay Pipe		Petersen 1963	29/32" widest diameter
Iron Scissors	MS3.C1L56.3	Grange 1987	5 3/32" long
Navy Button	FMW.317	Branstner & Branstner 2002 Dunnigan 1980 Albert 1976	23/32" diameter
Light Artillery Button	FMW.385	Branstner & Branstner 2002 Dunnigan 1975 Wright 1985 Grange 1987	25/32" diameter
6th Regiment Button	FMW.353	Branstner & Branstner 2002 Campbell 1965 Dunnigan 1975	5/8" diameter
16th Regiment Button	FMW.294	Branstner & Branstner 2002 Campbell 1965 Dunnigan 1975 Grange 1987	5/8" diameter
Riflemen Button	FMW.353	Branstner & Branstner 2002 Campbell 1965 Grange 1987	25/32" diameter
Artillery Button	FMW.296	Branstner & Branstner 2002 Dunnigan 1975 Grange 1987	9/15" diameter
Brass British Hat Plate	MS3.C1H15.5	Dunnigan 1980 Grange 1987	3 1/4" x 1 3/4"
Brass U.S. Infantry Hat Plate	MS3.C1B15.1	Grange 1987 Emerson 1996	1 5/8" x 2 5/8"
Leather Shoe Sole	MS3.C1D8.43	Grange 1987	7 5/8" long 2 1/16" heel length 1 15/16" heel width
Iron Boot Heel Plate	MS3.C1D8.44	Grange 1987	2 23/32" total length 2 5/16" outside width-open end

Artifact	Catalog Number	Reference	Dimensions
Bone Button Blank	MS3.C1H44.31	Grange 1987	1 29/32" long 13/16" wide 1/16" thick
Hand-Painted Pearlware Pitcher	MS3.C1D6.2 MS3.C1E5.1 MS3.C1E7		6 3/8" high
Microscope Lens	MS3.C1A3.1	Grange 1987	5/8" maximum diameter
Bone Knife	FMW.135	Branstner & Branstner 2002	1 29/32" long 11/32" wide
Ink Bottle	1997.1.64	Brose 1967 Carter 2001 Antique Bottle Collectors Haven 2002	2 19/32" high 2 17/32" base diameter
Coffee Mill Plate	MS3.E1Q19.1	Stewart 1998 Mark Good 2002 (pers. comm.) Judith Sivonda 2002 (pers. comm.) Mike White 2002 (pers. comm.)	1 7/8" x 1 9/32"
Champagne Bottle	MS3.A7A8.1	Wright 1985	9 9/16" high 2 3/4" base diameter
General Service Button	MS3.E1Y7.1	Johnson 1948 Stewart 1998 Grange 1999	2 7/32" diameter
Brass Helmet Spike	MS4.L5.1	Brose 1967 Howell 1975 Emerson 1996	3 1/4" high
Brass Helmet Spike Base	MS4.L8.3	Brose 1967 Howell 1975 Emerson 1996	3 15/32" wide
Duffy's Malt Whiskey Bottle	U.1922	Brose 1967	10 1/2" high 3" base diameter
U.S.Q.M.D. Plate	1997.1.70	Brose 1967	9 5/8" diameter
U.S.Q.M.D. Tumblers	1997.1.63 1997.1.64	Brose 1967 Lockhart 2002	2 5/8" base diameter 14 facets
National Park Drug Store Bottle	MS4.1.0.1	Brose 1967	4 3/32" high 1 25/32" base diameter
1895 Penny	MS3.E1M4.1	Grange 1999	3/4" diameter 1/16" thick
"DEUX LOUTRE" Lead Token	FMW.132	Branstner & Branstner 2002	1 11/16" x 1 5/8" 3/16" thick

APPENDIX II:
Archaeology and the
Mackinac Island State Park Commission

In 1959 Dr. Eugene Petersen, director of historic projects for the Mackinac Island State Park Commission [MISPC], contracted with Dr. Moreau Maxwell of Michigan State University [MSU] to carry out a season of archaeological excavation at Michilimackinac. Thus began an archaeological project that has continued every summer since then, one of the longest on-going projects of its kind.

The French established Michilimackinac around 1714. It passed into British control in 1761 as a result of the fall of New France the previous year. By the time the British abandoned the site for Mackinac Island in 1781, the small fort and mission had grown into a sizable fortified trading settlement, including nearly 100 houses outside the palisade. Michilimackinac was abandoned in response to George Rogers Clark's successes in the Illinois country during the American Revolution. Fearing that the Americans would advance north, Lieutenant Governor Patrick Sinclair decided to relocate his garrison from a wood fort on an exposed point to a stone fort on a hill on an island. Fort Mackinac, on Mackinac Island, was built between 1779 and 1781. Many buildings were moved from the mainland seven miles across water or ice to the new fort and village below. Archaeological evidence shows that what was left after the move was demolished so that the old fort could not be used as a staging ground to attack the new one.

The tip-of-the-mitt was essentially abandoned for nearly one hundred years, until the coming of the railroad. In 1857, however, a developer named Edgar Conkling platted Mackinaw City and set aside the site of the old fort as a public park. The Conkling plat was followed when Mackinaw City was finally settled in the 1880s.

In 1904 the city gave the park to the state, which turned Michilimackinac State Park over to the Park Commission in 1909. The wooded beach was a favorite local picnic spot, and with the advent of the automobile a popular campground developed. During the Great Depression, the park was the site of a public works project, and the palisade was reconstructed in its historic location, as determined by digging for remnants of the original posts. A few cabins were built inside the fort. By 1959 the reconstruction was in need of major repair.

The restoration of Fort Mackinac, begun in 1958, was a huge success and the commission turned its attention to its mainland park. Unlike Fort Mackinac, with its many historic buildings, nothing historic remained on the surface at Michilimackinac. That is why Dr. Petersen brought in an archaeological team. The first season was very productive. The Provision Storehouse, Commanding Officer's House, traders' houses and Soldiers' Barracks were located and approximately 20,000 artifacts were recovered (Maxwell and Binford 1961). The barracks building was reconstructed, furnished as a museum and opened to the public in 1960. This pattern of excavation and reconstruction continued through the 1960s, and much of the west half of the fort was excavated and rebuilt.

One particularly innovative exhibit was the archaeology tunnel. This underground exhibit shows the remains of an original root cellar and French-era well preserved in place, as well as providing display space for the most interesting and complete of the nearly one million artifacts recovered to date. Accessed through a reconstructed trader's house, this modern museum does not detract from the historic setting above ground. The original archaeology tunnel opened in 1962. The exhibit, except for the original ruins, was completely re-designed and updated in 1992.

By 1969 it was apparent that overseeing archaeology at Michilimackinac was a full-time job, not one that could be split with academic responsibilities. Lyle Stone, whose doctoral dissertation summarized the first ten years of excavation at Michilimackinac, was hired as the commission's first staff archaeologist, with oversight of archaeology at all MISPC parks. His revised dissertation, jointly published by the MISPC and MSU, became one of the standard artifact identification sources in the relatively new field of historical archaeology (Stone 1974).

At about this time, a new Visitor's Center under the Mackinac Bridge was planned for Michilimackinac. Preliminary excavations revealed remains of a colonial structure and several summers were spent excavating the remains of three rowhouses from the suburbs of the fort (Stone 1973).

In 1974 excavation resumed inside the fort walls. Leaving the west side behind, archaeologists began work on the powder magazine, which turned out to be the most intact building ruin at Michilimackinac (Heldman and Minnerly 1977). It was built underground to contain possible explosions. When its wooden walls were set on fire during the final demolition of the fort, they caved in and the overlying sod roof collapsed, extinguishing the fire and preserving the charred wood floor.

During this excavation, the archaeology program underwent several changes. Dr. Stone left to pursue career opportunities in Arizona and was replaced by Dr. Donald Heldman. Also during this time the commission acquired its own laboratory and storage space in Lansing and reclaimed the artifacts MSU had been housing since 1959.

During Dr. Heldman's twenty-year tenure, his Michilimackinac efforts were concentrated on the southeast quadrant of the fort. In addition to completing the powder magazine, he directed the excavation of multiple units of the Southeast and South Southeast Rowhouses, most notably the home of Ezekiel Solomon, Michigan's first Jewish settler (Halchin 1985; Heldman 1977, 1978, 1984, 1986 1991; Heldman and Grange 1981). Advances in recovery technique, such as water screening, led to more artifacts and information being discovered, but slowed the pace of excavation.

Dr. Heldman also created the *Archaeological Completion Report Series* within the commission's vibrant publication program. This series of technical monographs has allowed the results of the MISPC's archaeology program to be shared quickly with other archaeologists and interested members of the public. Topics have included site reports for projects throughout the Straits of Mackinac region (Evans 2001; Grange 1987; Halchin 1985; Heldman 1977, 1978, 1983; Heldman and Grange 1981; Martin 1985; Prahl and Branstner 1984), detailed artifact studies (Adams 1989; Frurip et al. 1983; Hauser 1982; Hamilton & Emery 1988), and other specialized archaeological projects (Morand 1994; Scott 1985; Whitaker 1998; Williams and Shapiro 1982).

Upon Dr. Heldman's retirement in 1995, he was replaced by Dr. Lynn Morand (later Lynn Evans). She finished excavating a house in the Southeast Row House, and has returned to the west side of the fort to complete the South Southwest Row House and tie together current results with excavations done over thirty years ago (Evans 2001, 2002).

Although Michilimackinac is the primary focus of the MISPC's archaeology program, it is not the sole focus. In 1972 three amateur archaeologists and historians from Cheboygan, Ellis and Mary Olson and Margaret Lentini, rediscovered the site of Michigan's first industrial complex, now known as Historic Mill Creek. In the 1780s Robert Campbell established this sawmill, gristmill and farm, located four miles east of Mackinaw City. After Campbell's death Michael Dousman operated the complex through the 1830s. Following the settling of Cheboygan, which had a more dependable source of waterpower, the Mill Creek mills were abandoned. The property was tenant farmed, quarried for limestone, and had reverted back to state forest by the time the site was rediscovered.

Excavations carried out in 1973, 1974 and 1975 revealed the remains of the dam, a Campbell-era house and separate workshop and a Dousman-era house and forge combined in one building (Martin 1985). Following the transfer of the land to the MISPC in 1975, additional excavations, carried out in 1979 and 1980, enabled the dam and sawmill to be reconstructed before the new park was opened to the public in 1984 (Ford 1979, 1980). Between 1984 and 1994 the excavation of the American Millwright's House was completed and additional work was done on the Campbell House and two unidentified structures in the historic area (Kempton 1986, Scott 1994). During this time the British Workshop was reconstructed based on archaeological evidence. The American Millwright's House and Forge is currently being rebuilt around its preserved double fireplace.

The MISPC also carried out numerous archaeology projects on Mackinac Island. Although Fort Mackinac retains the buildings standing when the army turned it over to the state in 1895, some structures had come and gone during the fort's 114-year military service.

The earliest of these, and the first to be excavated, was the well dug by the British during the fort's construction. The well failed before 1812, and was filled in fits and starts over the rest of the fort's history. A 1965 University of Michigan archaeological team carried out initial testing for the well (Brose 1966). It was definitely located and more completely excavated by a University of South Florida (USF) field school under the direction of Dr. Roger Grange, Jr. in 1980 and 1981 (Wright 1985).

For several summers Dr. Grange and USF field schools excavated at Fort Mackinac, including the Provision Storehouse, the East Blockhouse and the blacksmith shops (Grange 1987, 1997, 1999; Stewart 1998). They also excavated in a standing building when the floor of the Officers' Wood Quarters was lifted in 1986 (Clifford 1990). Crawl spaces and other nooks have yielded numerous interesting finds stashed by soldiers over the years (Petersen 1963, 1972).

The MISPC has carried out archaeological excavations at sites outside Fort Mackinac as well. The 1965 University of Michigan Mackinac Island project, under the direction of Dr. James Fitting and David Brose, excavated part of the Custer Road dump (Brose 1967). This dump, one of many on the island, was used by the soldiers at Fort Mackinac and the artifacts in it shed more light on their personal lives.

The Biddle House, one of the oldest homes on Mackinac Island, was restored in the 1950s. It is owned by the MISPC and open to the public in the summer. In 1972 one of its early privies was discovered and excavated during the restoration of a later privy (Stone 1975). It turned out to contain a fabulous collection of early nineteenth-century ceramics, which tell much about civilian island life and make an interesting comparison to the Mill Creek collection.

The most recent archaeological project at Fort Mackinac was the testing and excavation associated with the repair of the Fort Mackinac wall. This project, directed by Mark Branstner of Great Lakes Research, included the excavation of a nineteenth-century drainage system on the parade ground (Branstner and Branstner 2002).

Archaeology has a long history in the Straits of Mackinac and has made many contributions to our understanding and presentation of history at Mackinac State Historic Parks. A long-standing goal was met in 2001 with the completion of the Eugene and Marian Petersen Archaeology and History Center in Mackinaw City. For the first time, all of the MISPC archaeological records, artifacts and photographs are housed at the Straits of Mackinac, rather than in Lansing.

Several areas have been set aside within Michilimackinac as archaeological preserves, but there are still many more areas to be excavated and reconstructed. Because of the straits' rich history, all of our sites have archaeological potential. Archaeology is an adventure. Every day holds the chance to find a new piece of history. Who knows what stories remain to be uncovered?

REFERENCES CITED

Adams, Diane L.
    1989   Lead Seals from Fort Michilimackinac, 1715-1781. *Archaeological Completion Report Series* No. 14.
                      Mackinac State Historic Parks [MSHP], Mackinac Island, Michigan.

Albert, Alphaeus H.
    1976   *Record of American Uniform and Historical Buttons* (Bicentennial Edition). Boyertown Publishing
                      Company, Boyertown, Pennsylvania.

Antique Bottle Collectors Haven
    2002   Antique Ink Bottles.
                      <http://www.antiquebottles.com/ink/index.html>.

Askin, John
    1776   1776 Inventory. Askin Family Papers. Manuscript Group 19, A3, National Archives of Canada, Ottawa.
                      Copy on file, MSHP, Mackinaw City, Michigan.

Branstner, Mark C., and Christine N. Branstner
    2002   The Fort Mackinac Wall Restoration and Improvement Projects, Mackinac Island, Michigan: The 2000
                      and 2001 Field Seasons. GLRA Report No. 2002-03. Report Submitted by Great Lakes Research Inc. to
                      Mackinac State Historic Parks.

Brose, David
    1966   Excavations in Fort Mackinac, 1965. *Michigan Archaeologist* 12(2):88-101.

    1967   The Custer Road Dump Site: An Exercise in Victorian Archaeology. *Michigan Archaeologist*
                      13(2):37-128.

Brown, Margaret Kimball
    1971   Glass from Fort Michilimackinac: A Classification System for Eighteenth Century Glass.
                      Michigan Archaeologist 17(3-4):97-215.

Campbell, J. Duncan
    1965   Military Buttons: Long-lost heralds of Fort Mackinac's past. *Mackinac History* I:7. Mackinac Island
                      State Park Commission [MISPC], Mackinac Island, Michigan.

Carter, Michael
    2001   The Carter Pen: An Ink Manufacturer's Dream. Pen Collectors of America.
                      <http://www.pencollectors.com/pennant/fall99/carter.html>.

Cleland, Charles E.
    1971   (editor) The Lasanen Site: An Historic Burial Locality in Mackinac County, Michigan.
                      Anthropological Series Vol. 1 No. 1. Michigan State University Museum, East Lansing.

    1972   From Sacred to Profane: Style Drift in the Decoration of Jesuit Finger Rings. *American Antiquity*
                      37(2):202-210.

Clifford, Laura Dee
 1990   Excavations at the Officers' Wooden Quarters at Fort Mackinac, Michigan. Master's thesis, Department of Anthropology, University of South Florida, Tampa.

Coysh, A.W. and R.K. Henrywood
 1982   *The Dictionary of Blue and White Printed Pottery 1780-1880.* Antique Collectors' Club, Woodbridge, Suffolk.

Dunnigan, Brian Leigh
 1973   King's Men at Mackinac: The British Garrisons, 1780-1796. *Reports in Mackinac History and Archaeology* No. 3. MISPC, Mackinac Island, Michigan.

 1975   Milestones from the Past: Military Buttons and Insignia from Mackinac. *Mackinac History* II(2). MISPC, Mackinac Island, Michigan.

 1980   The British Army at Mackinac: 1812-1815. *Reports in Mackinac History and Archaeology* No. 7. MISPC, Mackinac Island, Michigan.

Emerson, William K.
 1996   *Encyclopedia of United State Army Insignia and Uniforms.* University of Oklahoma Press, Norman.

Evans, Lynn L.M.
 2001   House D of the Southeast Row House: Excavations at Fort Michilimackinac, 1989-1997. *Archaeological Completion Report Series* No. 17. MSHP, Mackinac Island, Michigan.

 2002   Recent Archaeology at Michilimackinac: The Archaeology of Fur Traders and Archaeologists. Paper presented at the 35th Conference of the Society for Historical Archaeology, Mobile, Alabama.

Ford, Thomas B.
 1979   Archaeological Investigations at the Mill Creek (Filbert) Site. Submitted to the MISPC as Partial Fulfillment of Contract #LRP98, Mill Creek Development, Coastal Management Program, Division of Land Resource Programs, DNR, State of Michigan.

 1980   Archaeological Investigations at the Mill Creek (Filbert) Site: 1980 Season. Submitted to the MISPC.

Fortier, Margaret, translator
 n.d.   Records of the royal notary at Fort Michilimackinac, August 1, 1754 to July 30, 1766. Transcript on file, MSHP, Mackinaw City, Michigan. Original in Thomas Gage Papers, William L. Clements Library, University of Michigan, Ann Arbor, Michigan.

Frurip, David J., Russell Malewicki and Donald P. Heldman
 1983   Colonial Nails from Michilimackinac: Differentiation by Chemical and Statistical Analysis. *Archaeological Completion Report Series* No. 7. MISPC, Mackinac Island, Michigan.

Gérin-Lajoie, Marie, translator and editor
 1976   Fort Michilimackinac in 1749: Lotbinière's Plan and Description. *Mackinac History* II(5). MISPC, Mackinac Island, Michigan.

Grange, Roger T., Jr.
 1987   Excavations at Fort Mackinac, 1980-1982: The Provision Storehouse. *Archaeological Completion Report Series* No. 12. MISPC, Mackinac Island, Michigan.

 1997   Pathways to the East Blockhouse at Fort Mackinac. Manuscript, MSHP, Mackinaw City, Michigan.

 1999   The Excavation of the Blacksmith Shops at Fort Mackinac. Manuscript, MSHP, Mackinaw City, Michigan.

Halchin, Jill Y.

    1985   Excavations at Fort Michilimackinac, 1983-1985: House C of the Southeast Rowhouse, The Solomon-Levy-Parant House. *Archaeological Completion Report Series* No. 11. MISPC, Mackinac Island, Michigan.

Hamilton, T.M.

    1976   Firearms on the Frontier: Guns at Fort Michilimackinac 1715-1781. *Reports in Mackinac History and Archaeology* No. 5. MISPC, Mackinac Island, Michigan.

Hamilton, T.M. and K.O. Emery

    1988   Eighteenth Century Gunflints from Fort Michilimackinac and Other Colonial Sites. *Archaeological Completion Report Series* No. 13. MISPC, Mackinac Island, Michigan.

Hauser, Judith Ann

    1982   Jesuit Rings from Fort Michilimackinac and Other European Contact Sites. *Archaeological Completion Report Series* No. 5. MISPC, Mackinac Island, Michigan.

Heldman, Donald P.

    1977   Excavations at Fort Michilimackinac, 1976: The Southeast and South Southeast Row Houses. *Archaeological Completion Report Series* No. 1. MISPC, Mackinac Island, Michigan.

    1978   Excavations at Fort Michilimackinac, 1977: House One of the South Southeast Row House. *Archaeological Completion Report Series* No. 2. MISPC, Mackinac Island, Michigan.

    1980   Coins at Michilimackinac. *Historical Archaeology* 14:82-107.

    1983   Archaeological Investigations at French Farm Lake in Northern Michigan, 1981-1982. *Archaeological Completion Report Series* No. 6. MISPC, Mackinac Island, Michigan.

    1984   East Side, West Side, All Around the Town: Stratigraphic Alignment and Resulting Settlement Patterns at Fort Michilimackinac, 1715-1781. Paper presented at the 17th Conference of the Society for Historical Archaeology, Williamsburg, Virginia.

    1986   Michigan's First Jewish Settlers: A View from the Solomon-Levy Trading House at Fort Michilimackinac, 1765-1781. *Journal of New World Archaeology* 6(4):21-33.

    1991   The French in Michigan and Beyond: An Archaeological View from Fort Michilimackinac Toward the West. In *French Colonial Archaeology: The Illinois Country and the Western Great Lakes*, John A. Walthall, editor, pp. 201-217. University of Illinois Press, Urbana.

Heldman, Donald P. and Roger T. Grange, Jr.

    1981   Excavations at Fort Michilimackinac 1978-79: The Rue de la Babillarde. *Archaeological Completion Report Series* No. 3. MISPC, Mackinac Island, Michigan.

Heldman, Donald P. and William L. Minnerly

    1977   The Powder Magazine at Fort Michilimackinac: Excavation Report. *Reports in Mackinac History and Archaeology* No. 6. MISPC, Mackinac Island, Michigan.

Henry, Alexander

    1809   *Travels and Adventures in Canada and the Indian Territories, between the years 1760 and 1776.* I. Riley, New York. University Microfilms, *March of America Facsimile Series* No. 43, 1966.

Howell, Edgar M.
    1975   United States Army Headgear 1855-1902: Catalog of United States Army Uniforms in the Collections of the Smithsonian Institution, II. *Smithsonian Studies in History and Technology* No. 30. Smithsonian Institution Press, Washington, D.C.

Johnson, David F.
    1948   *Uniform Buttons: American Armed Forces 1784-1948*, Vol. I. Century House, Watkins Glen, N.Y.

Judge Advocate General
    1888   General Court Martial of Frank Darlington, Fort Mackinac, November 23, 1888. Records of the Judge Advocate General (Army), Record Group 153, National Archives, Washington, D.C.

Kalm, Peter
    1987   *Peter Kalm's Travels in North America: The English Version of 1770*, revised from the original Swedish and edited by Adolph B. Benson. Dover Publications, New York.

Kempton, Karen L.
    1986   Archaeological Investigations at Old Mill Creek: An Early 19th Century Residence at the Straits of Mackinac. Master's thesis, Department of Anthropology, University of South Florida, Tampa.

Lockhart, Bill <lockhart@NMSUA.NMSU.EDU>
    2002   Re: Sun Colored Amethyst Glass. <HISTARCH@asu.edu>. 28 January.

Lorenzini, Michele and Karlis Karklins
    2000-2001 Man-in the Moon Beads. *Beads* 12-13:39-47.

Lowrie, Walter, editor
    1832a   *American state papers.* Public lands 1. Gates and Seaton, Washington, D.C.

    1832b   *American state papers.* Public lands 5. Gates and Seaton, Washington, D.C.

Martin, Patrick Edward
    1985   The Mill Creek Site and Pattern Recognition in Historical Archaeology. *Archaeological Completion Report Series* No. 10. MISPC, Mackinac Island, Michigan.

Maxwell, Moreau S.
    1964   Indian Artifacts at Fort Michilimackinac, Mackinaw City, Michigan. *Michigan Archaeologist* 10(2):23-30.

Maxwell, Moreau S. and Lewis Binford
    1961   Excavations at Fort Michilimackinac, Mackinac City, Michigan, 1959 Season. *Publications of the Museum, Michigan State University, Cultural Series* Vol. 1, No. 1. East Lansing.

May, George S., editor
    1960   *The Doctor's Secret Journal.* MISPC, Mackinac Island, Michigan.

McCrae, David
    1777-1787 David McCrae and Co., of Michilimackinac accts. with Wm. and John Kay of Montreal, 1777-1787. Quebec Papers, Vol.B, 75:170-241. Toronto Public Libraries, Toronto. Copy on file, MSHP, Mackinaw City, Michigan.

Michigan Pioneer and Historical Society

    1888   *Historical Collections* vol. xii. Thorp and Godfrey, Lansing.

    1903   *Pioneer Collections* vol. iii. Robert Smith Printing Company, Lansing.

    1909   *Historical Collections* vol.xv. Wynkoop Hallenbeck Crawford Company, Lansing.

Miller, J. Jefferson, II and Lyle M. Stone

    1970   Eighteenth-Century Ceramics from Fort Michilimackinac: A Study in Historical Archaeology. *Smithsonian Studies in History and Technology* No. 4. Smithsonian Institution Press, Washington.

Morand, Lynn L.

    1994   Craft Industries at Fort Michilimackinac, 1715-1781. *Archaeological Completion Report Series* No. 15. MSHP, Mackinac Island, Michigan.

Neumann, George C. and Frank J. Kravic

    1975   *Collector's Illustrated Encyclopedia of the American Revolution.* Stackpole Books, Harrisburg, Pennsylvania.

Petersen, Eugene T.

    1963   Clay Pipes: A Footnote to Mackinac's History. *Mackinac History* I:1. MISPC, Mackinac Island, Michigan.

    1972   The Preservation of History at Mackinac. *Reports in Mackinac History and Archaeology* No. 2. MISPC, Mackinac Island, Michigan.

Prahl, Earl and Mark Branstner

    1984   Archaeological Investigations on Mackinac Island 1983: The Watermain and Sewer Project. *Archaeological Completion Report Series* No. 8. MISPC, Mackinac Island, Michigan.

Quaife, Milo M., editor

    1928   *The John Askin Papers, 1747-1795* vol. 1. Burton Historical Records. Detroit Library Commission, Detroit.

Rinehart, Charles J.

    1990   Crucifixes and Medallions: Their Role at Fort Michilimackinac. *Volumes in Historical Archaeology* XI. The South Carolina Institute of Archaeology and Anthropology, University of South Carolina, Columbia.

Scott, Elizabeth M.

    1985   French Subsistence at Fort Michilimackinac, 1715-1781: The Clergy and the Traders. *Archaeological Completion Report Series* No. 9. MISPC, Mackinac Island, Michigan.

    1991   *Such Diet as Befitted His Station as Clerk: The Archaeology of Subsistence and Cultural Diversity at Fort Michilimackinac, 1761-1781.* Doctoral dissertation, Department of Anthropology, University of Minnesota. University Microfilms International, Ann Arbor.

    1994   Looking at Gender and More: Feminist Archaeology and a 19th-Century Millwright's House. Paper presented at the 27th Conference of the Society for Historical Archaeology, Vancouver, British Columbia.

Stewart, Sheila K.

    1998   The Third Blacksmith Shop at Fort Mackinac, Michigan, 1858-circa 1875. Master's thesis, Department of Anthropology, University of South Florida, Tampa.

Stone, Lyle M.

    1973   Fort Michilimackinac-Parking Lot Area: Summary of Excavations and Structural Evidence, 1970-73. Manuscript, MSHP, Mackinaw City, Michigan.

    1974   Fort Michilimackinac, 1715-1781: An Archaeological Perspective on the Revolutionary Frontier. *Anthropological Series,* Vol. 2. Michigan State University, East Lansing, in cooperation with MISPC, Mackinac Island, Michigan.

    1975   The Biddle-john Site: An Early Nineteenth Century Outhouse on Mackinac Island Michigan. Manuscript, MSHP, Mackinaw City, Michigan.

Stuart, Charles

    1959   Locks. In *The Concise Encyclopedia of Antiques* vol. 4, L.G.G. Ramsey, editor, pp. 273-277. Hawthorn Books, New York.

Thwaites, Reuben Gold, editor

    1910   *Wisconsin Historical Collections* vol. xix. State Historical Society of Wisconsin, Madison.

Wallace, W. Stewart, editor

    1934   *Documents Relating to the Northwest Company*. The Champlain Society, Toronto.

Whitaker, John M.F.

    1998   The Functions of Four Colonial Yards of the Southeast Row House, Fort Michilimackinac, Michigan. *Archaeological Completion Report Series* No. 16. MSHP, Mackinac Island, Michigan.

Williams, J. Mark and Gary Shapiro

    1982   A Search for Eighteenth Century Village at Michilimackinac: A Soil Resistivity Survey. *Archaeological Completion Report Series* No. 4. MISPC, Mackinac Island, Michigan.

Wright, Robin

    1985   The 1780 British Well Site. Master's thesis, Department of Anthropology, University of South Florida, Tampa.

ACKNOWLEDGEMENTS

I am deeply indebted to many people who made this book possible. Dr. Eugene Petersen's vision brought archaeology to Mackinac. Countless archaeologists have worked on MISPC sites over the past forty-four seasons to uncover the artifacts and ruins on these pages. I particularly acknowledge Drs. Lyle Stone and Donald Heldman, my predecessors as staff archaeologist, who directed most of these projects.

Many fellow MSHP staff have helped me with this book. Dr. David Armour, who first came to Mackinac in 1965 to work with the archaeology program, suggested artifacts and made many helpful comments on the text and captions, as did Phil Porter and William Fritz. Steve Brisson and Carl Nold provided thoughtful reviews of the draft, as did Tim Putman, who also located many modern park images. William Fritz conserved many of the artifacts, and along with David Kronberg, Larry Young and Michelle Hill, dismantled and reassembled numerous exhibits so artifacts could be photographed. Many other staff members provided encouragement through their interest in the project and I thank them all, especially Jim Evans, my husband and coworker.

Dr. Roger T. Grange, Jr., made valuable suggestions regarding Fort Mackinac archaeology and artifacts.

In addition to people cited elsewhere, the following people personally shared their expertise: Steven Baule on the Royal Irish regiment; Brother Jim Boynton, S.J., on Jesuit iconography; Mark Good, Judith Sivonda and Mike White on Parker coffee mills.

John Wooden photographed all of the artifacts. David Woods did other special project photography. Fran Russell and Group 230 designed the book.

Despite the efforts of all of these people, there may be errors in this volume and they are my responsibility.

Special thanks go to the Mackinac Associates, friends of MSHP in many ways, who sponsored this project in honor of their twentieth anniversary.

Lynn L.M. Evans
April 2003

ABOUT THE AUTHOR

Lynn L. M. Evans is the Curator of Archaeology for Mackinac State Historic Parks, a position she has held since 1996. She began excavating at Michilimackinac in 1989 while conducting research on frontier craft industries. A native of Cincinnati, Lynn holds a B.A. in anthropology and museum studies from Beloit College (1987) and a Ph.D. in American Civilization – Historical Archaeology from the University of Pennsylvania (1993). She resides with her husband, Jim, in Mackinaw City.